Trapped

by

Evil

Allison D. Walls

ISBN-13: 978-0692819371 (Allison D. Walls)

ISBN-10: 0692819371

© 2016

Credits

    Editor: Anna L. Walls

    Cover: Rachel A. Olson

God has placed many people in my path, and for that I am most thankful. My youngest brother and his wife, my neighbor, and my best girlfriend from high school, and all my Sisters in Christ who prayed for me along the way, I thank them most for believing me when things were most unbelievable. Most important to my journey, I am most grateful to a fantastic healer who healed me and helps me still as I struggle to continue my life. I also thank my editor, and Facebook friend, Anna, another editor, Dawn, and my cover artist, Rachel. God set them all in my path so his will could be done in publishing this book and helping me help other people who might be having similar problems.

Introduction

I have been through a lot of different situations with family, friends, jobs, and just everyday living, before I put all the pieces of the puzzle together and figured out that all my problems were not of my own making. Someone had done something to me, something wrong and terrifyingly evil. Today I thank the Lord, who sent me the people to help me, and the work done to heal me and to deliver me from all destruction. It says in **Romans 10:17** *"Faith comes by hearing, and hearing by the word of God."* So dear Father as in **Romans 12:1** *"I present my body a living sacrifice, holy, acceptable unto you God."* I have always asked for forgiveness of all my sins, those I am aware of and those I am not aware of. He said in **Psalm 103:3** that you *"forgive all my sins, and heals all my diseases."* I thank you Father that you will satisfy me with a long life.

Sickness, I command you to never come near me, in the name of Jesus Christ, and for me to be able to help myself and others by praying in the name of Jesus, that the demonic helpers and symptoms never try to come near me. I cover myself always with the shed blood of Jesus Christ. I

1

receive my healing and I am healed in the name of Jesus Christ of Nazareth, because **Jeremiah 30:17** tells me that *"my health is restored and my wounds are healed."* I will always keep my eyes focused on the cross and not on the circumstances, and will continue to thank Him, praise Him and repeat His work and His promises back to Him.

I saw a full and complete manifestation of my healing. I will not be discouraged. As it says in **2 Corinthians 1:2** *"For all the promises of God in him are Yea, and Amen."* Remember our God is a God of wonders and miracles; believe and receive. I believe healing is for everyone. I will always plead the blood of Jesus on my home and family, my mind and body, my actions and my every word. Your word of promise tells me in **Psalm 118:17** *"I shall not die, but live, and declare the works of the Lord."*

No one knows but the Lord what I went through. But it's over, and can never in the name of Jesus be on me or in me ever again. I thank you, Lord, for letting me be the person that I am. I can pray for hours, for myself and others. I love to pray and help people. Whatever their needs are, I know that if the God I know can heal me the way He did, He will do anything in His will for me and others in need.

God was able to help me, and I know he can help others too. If I hadn't sought God, I know I would have died. My problems, as you will read, had the doctors baffled. Because of what I have been though, I can say this to everyone, 'never eat or drink unless you know who gave it to you and where it came from'. There are people who work evil witchcraft and put things in the drinks or food to make you sick, and I'm not talking about some kind of date rape drug, I'm talking about something much more evil. I was very sick and confused until God healed me. I think of this often, and I thank God for saving my life.

Thanks be to God!

Romans 15:33 "Now the God of peace be with you all. Amen."

Here, I give you the story of my life that you may find your way past the hazards of your life sooner than I did.

Trapped by Evil

Chapter 1

My mom met my dad sometime in early 1951, and in February of 1952 my oldest brother was born. My dad did right by my mom, and in December they became a larger family of three. One day my mom's grandma showed up with a five-year-old girl, my mom's oldest daughter. Dad was furious; mom hadn't told him about any other kids, but she'd been scared to; she knew she would never find a husband if she was bringing a kid along. He wasn't mad at my sister though; it wasn't her fault her dad had run off before she was born, but it was always a sore point between my mom and dad.

Two years later another boy was brought into our family, and two years after that, I was born in March of 1956.

My dad did his best for all of us, and he never treated my sister any different than the rest of us.

When I was four, my dad brought us home a puppy. I named her Peanut. She was my best buddy; I loved her so much. There weren't any kids in the neighborhood my age and I was too little to play with my brothers or my sister; now I had someone to play with.

I remember being so little that I couldn't reach the handles to turn on the water. The kitchen sink was so big, if I wanted a drink of water, I had to stand there and yell "Water" until someone came and got me some. I remember not being able to pronounce the word very well.

Another thing I remember back then was taking a bath in that sink; it made me feel special, just me and mama. I had long, dirty blond hair back then and after she washed it, she'd comb it out and tie it up in ties so it came out curly in the morning.

One night I forgot to spit out my gum before I went to bed, and it came out and got all in my hair. Mama took me to a lady down the street. The gum had tangled my hair so badly, that she had to cut most of it off.

When daddy got home, the first thing he said was, "Who did this to you?"

I pointed to mom, but then she told him all about the gum.

I remember such good things about my dad. He'd pull me in his lap and explain things carefully. Then he'd ask if I understood. He would keep explaining until he was sure I understood and said so. I'd say, "Yes sir. I do," if I understood.

When I was five, we lived in Winston Salem, on Ninth Street; we were close enough to the stores to walk there. Our house sat up on a nice hill and on the other end of the street, a train went by every day. The conductor would throw sticks of white chalk out the window when he saw kids. My sister would draw hopscotch on the sidewalk with the chalk, and her and her friends would play. She would only let me watch because I was too little to join in on the activities. She was fifteen then, ten years older than I was.

My two brothers would play football or army in the back yard, screaming and hollering and having so much fun, but mama wouldn't let me go near, not even to watch, afraid I'd get hurt.

One Saturday, dad walked with my sister and my oldest brother to town. He had somewhere else to go so he left them at a store. On the way home a man tried to attack them. My sister and my brother fought hard to get away, kicking and screaming and biting. They got away and ran all the way home as fast as they could. Later my sister went with dad to the police station and identified the man; he was sent to jail. Ever since then, whenever mom and dad went out at night, they'd tell us not to open the door for anyone.

Sometimes mama would take me to the store with her when she went shopping. She'd hold my hand tight and tell me not to pull away or I'd get a spanking.

I suppose I listened as well as any other kid. One time I got away from her in a lady's shop, the place was called Davis Department Store. I found the lady's hat department and I was in heaven; I love hats. I'd put one on and then another one and looked at myself in the big mirror. I suppose I was making something of a mess, but I just couldn't help myself.

Then I heard, "Allison Dawn!" Mama was calling me and she was mad. She always used both my names when she was mad. I was going to get a whooping; I just knew it. She found me and she stood there with her fists on her hips. I just looked at her from behind the rim of the big hat I had on at the time. Then mama started laughing; it made me laugh too. She took the hat and put it back then we left. I guess being cute enough got me out of that butt whooping.

Saturdays were big for me. Dad would get me up early and I would eat breakfast with him and mama. I had three big choices to make every Saturday morning. Mom and dad both worked on Saturday, so I could choose to go to work with one or the other, or I could go to the Kitten Show with my sister and brothers. A lot of kids would go and dance on the stage and watch movies. Dad always gave me plenty of money to pay our way in, and to buy popcorn and drinks. My sister made me stay in my seat while she and my brothers went up on the stage to dance. She said I was too young. I didn't argue; I felt like I would get trampled if I went up there, everybody shaking their bodies and jumping around, doing the Twist, and the Jerk, and the Monkey to all to that loud rock and roll music. It was fun watching them though; I learned a lot of dance moves. To this day I love to dance – to shake a leg – when the music is rocking.

I liked going to work with mom or dad; I learned a lot. Dad worked at Craven's County Ham House. He cared a lot about his work, always being prompt and proper with the people who came in. He cut up all the meat, like big hogs, cows, and sometimes deer. When I went to work with dad, he would sit me on a stool and give me a small coke and some peanuts. I watched as he weighed the orders, wrapped it in white paper so quick, and then wrote the amount on the package with a marker. When the person was finished, he'd ring up the total on the cash register and put their packages in a brown bag. I always thought it looked like fun helping all those people. The line was always long, but my dad moved fast. He worked at the Ham House for thirty-seven and a half years.

Mom worked at H. Kress & Company 5.10.25 Cent Store. It was a department store. Everything was nice but cheap. First we would go to mama's hairdresser. This woman was tall and she always wore all white like a nurse in a hospital. I would watch every move as she washed mom's hair and fixed it up all pretty. Sometimes she'd get out those pink rods and give her a perm. I thought that was so interesting. One day, my hair was still short and mom said I could have a perm too. My hair came out with curls all over; I loved it.

After we were done at the beauty shop, we would go to work. I couldn't stay on the main floor where my mom worked; I had to sit in the break room and watch TV, color, or read. I met lots of the other workers there though, and I always got chocolate covered candy. Going to work with mama was boring, but I still liked it and learned a lot from all the different people.

While I was with mom or dad, my sister was supposed to be cleaning the house. My brothers would either sleep late or help her. They didn't want me there to be in the way.

One of the scariest things I can remember was an attempted break-in at our house. Mom and dad would go out at night sometimes, maybe once or twice a month, and leave us kids' home under the supervision of my sister. We'd usually watch TV until we went to bed. One such night we heard a car pull up outside and a man knocked on the door and asked if this was the Walls' house. Like dad always told us when they went out, we didn't say anything, staying real quiet by the TV. A few moments later, we heard him cutting away the screen from the window and trying to open it. I was scared to death, but none of us made a sound. Mom and dad came home just then and he ran off I guess. Daddy was the type of man to protect his family so they started looking for a different home.

We moved to a small town called Old Town, not too far away from our previous house. The new address was Speas Road, named after the folks we rented from. The house was much bigger, a two-story, colonial style home with lots, and I mean lots, of land.

I wasn't in school yet and I couldn't go to work with mom or dad anymore. When they both had to work on Saturday, my great aunt would come stay with me. I love her to no end; she was a diamond. She would go outside and pitch the softball for me to hit. If the walnuts were ready to crack, we would go collect them and we would make a walnut cake. It was hard getting enough walnuts for the cake because we'd be eating them too.

My great aunt was a God-fearing woman, and she taught me about God and the bible. She would always say, "Jesus loves you, Allison, and so do I."

In the afternoons, she would rock me in her lap singing, "*Jesus loves me, this I know, for the bible tells me so.*" This was the first song I learned about the Lord.

My great aunt would take me to church too. Every Sunday her husband would drive her over to pick me up and he would drop us off at the church. Sometimes he went in with us, but if he couldn't stay, he'd come back and pick us up after.

My great aunt was a wonderful lady. She could whip up a home-cooked meal in no time. My favorite was her homemade bread with butter and either grape jelly or apple butter.

My dad was raised on a farm not far from the Piedmont area. His dad died at fifty-two of a heart problem so his mom ran the farm and all thirteen of her children on her own. When we moved to this new house with all that land, dad planted a big garden. I swear we planted enough to feed an army, but somehow the army never showed up and it all got eaten.

I loved the garden. We grew all kinds of vegetables like green beans, tomatoes, potatoes, okra, peppers, cucumbers, corn, beets, squash, and melons. When dad came home from work, I was right on his tail. He would say, "Let's go look at the garden, Allison."

I learned a lot about the garden. He was always telling me "Don't step here or there." "Be careful, those are plants, not weeds."

When harvest time came around, it seemed like everything was done all at once, and mama would be canning the green beans, beets, tomatoes and corn. I would help as much as she would let me. She froze a lot of things too. My dad would say, "We're preparing for winter."

One day, dad brought home three goats. There was a big white billy goat—we called him Billy, a middle-sized black billy goat—we called him Blackie, and a small nanny goat—we called her Nanny. They were to keep the honeysuckle and kudzu vine under control. We kept them staked out around the garden wherever needed. I would move them to a new spot every day or so. We didn't just leave them to eat the weeds; we fed them grain too and I made sure they had plenty of water.

My favorite was Nanny. She would come sit on the front porch just like a person, she even jumped into the car once. Mama had a few beers too many so we took Nanny for a ride. It was so much fun watching as people looked twice or pointed. We never did it again; dad would have been upset at us if he found out.

My dad tried raising hogs one year too. He kept them in a big pen across the road. That fall a man came and they were butchered. He never did that again. Mama didn't care for them much at all.

We had chickens for a while too, some hens and a rooster. One summer a hen came out with some little ones. They were so cute and so tiny; I wanted to pick one up. All of a sudden the hen attacked me and got all in my long hair. Mama came running with her broom and knocked the hen out of my hair. I never tried to pick up one of her babies again, though I would help mom get the eggs every day. A fox started stealing all the eggs so we ended up giving the chickens away.

Billy, the big white billy goat got off his chain one time and we found him dead on our driveway. We don't know how he got loose or what happened to him. Dad said a car might have hit him, but it was impossible to tell. He dug a big hole down by the creek and put lots of rocks in the bottom. We then lined it real comfortable with hay and then covered him real warm with more. After we filled in the hole, we had a service for Mr. Billy White. I could tell daddy was sad; so was I. Dad always told me when something or someone passes away, it's one of the things in life we must all do. We didn't talk anymore about Mr. Billy White; it was too sad to talk about.

We had a really good life. We ate well because of the garden we had grown and because of where dad worked; he could 'bring home the bacon' in a very literal sense of the word. For us, junk food was popcorn on Sunday nights while we watched Bonanza on TV, or potato chips maybe over at a friend's house. Every day we got up to homemade biscuits, country ham, bacon or sausage, cream gravy and eggs. We never went to school hungry.

We never had a lot of money; we didn't have the best of things in our house, and dad didn't drive a brand new car, but we had lots of wonderful food. My mom was a great cook.

Chapter 2

Going to first grade didn't start out so well. I didn't want to go. I loved staying at home watching the I Love Lucy show every morning. Not liking my first grade teacher had a lot to do with it too.

Mrs. P___ was a large lady and she wore silk pantyhose with the line up the back. When she walked they rubbed together loudly. I made fun of her one day and she caught me. She made me go to the principal's office and they called my mom. I was sent home. All I did was imitate the noise she made when she walked. It made everyone laugh.

My mom wasn't too happy with me though. Mama said, "I didn't send you to school to be making fun of your teacher." I was grounded; I couldn't leave the yard or ride my bike for a few days, but I learned my lesson. I would never do that again. Nope, I did something else. I wasn't through with Mrs. P___ yet. I thought, *If first grade is like this, I will for sure hate school forever.*

Every time we had break, we would get ice cream in a cup or an ice cream sandwich. When Mrs. P___ ate her ice cream sandwich, she would roll her tongue up and down the middle of the sandwich, so I took it upon myself to start imitating her again. I showed all my classmates how she licked the ice cream out of her sandwich until she couldn't reach any more and then she'd bite the rest of it down in one big gulp. Everybody laughed, and of course she saw me and it was off to the principal's office again.

My backside got tore up that time, and it was a whole week of no bike and no going out of the yard. Worst of all, this time she told my dad. He gave me a real serious talking to, but later, when they thought I was sleeping, I heard them talking about me.

Dad said, "She's got to stop this."

Mom said, "I think it's that teacher. Allison doesn't know how to deal with her."

I didn't, and I didn't think the other kids did either.

My older brother was in the second grade and his classroom was right across the hall. One day I hid in his classroom, but he saw me and took me back to mine. My brother had a pretty teacher; I wanted to stay there.

I think Mrs. P___ didn't like me at all. She failed me that year. As soon as I realized what that meant, I was scared I'd have to go through it all again, but when I went back to school, I had a new teacher. Her name was Mrs.

C___; she was kind, pretty and I did really well in her class. I had lots of friends in school now. I love having friends.

My closest brother was in third grade now. His favorite thing to say to me was, "Be nice." He'd say, "Be nice, Al," when we got on the bus in the morning and any other time he saw me. He said it to me so much, a stranger would have thought it was my name. He was the best though; he always made sure I had money for ice cream at break.

Every morning my dad would get up about five in the morning and polish my shoes until they shined. Our driveway was just dirt so our shoes would get real muddy if we didn't walk through the grass coming and going from school. Since I loved playing kickball at school, I wore out my shoes often.

When the bus came, I would always start out the door with my coat under my arm because I didn't want my dress to get wrinkled. I ironed my own dress. If my dad saw, he would say, "Allison, get your coat on or you will catch a cold."

I helped my sister with the laundry every Saturday if I was home. Doing the laundry wasn't so bad though, we had a machine, but the wringer was broken, so my job was to hold a screwdriver in the screw while my sister rinsed the clothes. She would say, "Allison, do not move." If I did, the ringer bar would pop open and the clothes would be too wet to hang out on the line. In the winter we would hang them out anyway and they would freeze stiff. Sometimes the sun would dry them anyway. Most of my friends had a dryer, but we didn't.

There were other problems with our house besides the washer. We had an old Hot Point frig. It was small and the handle had come off at some point, so in order to open it, we kept a screwdriver lying on top. To open the door, we'd have to put the screwdriver into the hole where the handle was supposed to be and then hit it hard with the palm of our hand to trip the lock. We couldn't afford a new one and that was the only thing wrong with it. It kept our food good and cold all the time, so we kept it for years.

I spent the night at a girlfriend's house once. They lived pretty close to us. When I got home mama asked what we had for breakfast. I told her, we had a Pop-Tart, and before I could even tell her what a Pop-Tart was, she said it wasn't healthy so she cooked me up a big breakfast.

The only heat for the house was a coal stove in the living room. When we came home from school and the house was cold because mom and dad were both working, we had to gather small limbs to build a fire. One day my sister used an old bicycle tire. Boy, did that thing take off; that old coal stove turned completely red on the outside. We had lots of heat that day.

Some days she would use a spoonful of peanut butter on a napkin to light the fire. A few years later, we got an oil stove and that worked much better.

This old house didn't have heat upstairs so we all had electric blankets for winter; it was the best my folks could do. In the summer, it was real hot upstairs. That old house was good though. It might have been cold in the winter and hot in the summer, but it kept the rain off our heads.

Well, it did most of the time anyway. I remember one day; I was outside playing marbles with my brother when the sky started to get real dark. The winds picked up making the trees whip back and forth. Mama came home from work early that day and she called us to come inside. The rain came down, beating hard on the tin roof by the time we went to bed. We woke in the middle of the night to an odd sound; the tin roof had been rolled back and had fallen off into the front yard. Without the tin up there, rain was pouring in on us, so we ran downstairs and into rooms in the back of the house. The rain made a real mess of the living room and the kitchen. That was the worst thunderstorm I can remember. It scared my brothers too. To this day, big thunderstorms scare us some.

It took two weeks to fix the house and put a new roof up. The house was built in the nineteen hundreds. Dad paid $45 a month for us to live there. That might not sound like much by today's standards, but it was a lot for us back then.

In all, I thought life was pretty good, but mom and dad fought some. A lot of it was about my sister; dad resented that he was raising another man's child, and thought her father should help to pay some of the bills. It would go on and on, and round and round. They often said they were going to get a divorce once I graduated from high school. It made me wish they had put me in a children's home and get it over with. My mama took to drinking beer, though my dad did his share of drinking too.

Life went on though. When I was nine, and in third grade, my teacher was Mrs. W___. Things got really bad at home. My dad made it clear, that as soon as my sister was done with school, she could get a job over at the Hanes Plant making hose. What she made would help to pay the bills, but more than once he'd say she owed him for raising her, feeding and clothing her most of her life. She decided to get married instead. In her senior year, on her eighteenth birthday, she dressed up in a nice suit and told me at the bus stop that she wouldn't be back home. Her and her boyfriend had rented a trailer house in Clemmons; she finished high school at North Forsyth Senior High. When she moved out, I felt like I had lost a good friend.

Mama was pregnant that summer too. When mama was six months along, a man hit our car from the rear. I was there too, and my mama went into labor. My youngest brother was born on New Year's Day weighing only two pounds and thirteen ounces. He had to stay in the hospital for two months, until he gained enough weight to come home. Having a new baby in the family was a big change for me. Now there was a baby for me to help care for while they complained about my sister and not getting child support. I felt stuck taking care of him when mama would start drinking, or when she was cleaning the house or fixing meals. That baby was spoiled to no end. Some days I wanted to leave and not come back.

I went to work for my aunt and uncle on their tobacco farm. I made 75¢ an hour working in the barn handing tobacco to my aunt or cousin to tie onto tobacco sticks to be hung in the barn to dry out. They would then take the dry tobacco to the market to be weighed and sold. I saved all my money to buy pretty dresses to wear to school. My buying some of my school clothes helped my parents too. This also helped me learn the meaning of a dollar. It wasn't how much you made, it was how you spent the money you earned. It was wise to have something of value to show for the dollar you spent. It was hard work, but we had a lot of fun there too, telling jokes and playing jokes on each other.

My fourth grade teacher was with Mrs. C___. I had my hands full now. Now that my sister had moved out, it was up to me to do the chores at home. I'd learned to clean the house, make beds, wash the blinds, iron clothes, cook meals, all that, but now I was doing it all by myself, and there was my baby brother to take care of. Mama worked hard so someone had to mind the house. Come harvest time, I would help can up the vegetables or get them ready for the freezer.

I had a few friends that I liked to hang out with. My baby brother never wanted me to leave though. Because of him being born so early, he couldn't hear and had to wear hearing aids. He had to go to a special school to learn sign language. And because he couldn't hear very well, he would yell and kick and scream real loud if he knew I was planning to go somewhere without him. Sometimes he would run to the door and push it closed when I was on my way out.

I would get on my bike with Peanut running along beside. Sometimes I would go to the drug store, a place called Crown Pharmacy. It was right next to the doctor's office. Everyone went there for everything. It even had a snack bar where you could have a hotdog or hamburger and fries. Sometimes I would go there after school to have a snack, but not very often. If my mom found out that I used my lunch money there instead of for lunch at school, I was in real trouble with her.

Another place I liked to go was the Dairy Queen. They had really good hotdogs and fries, and were well known for their ice cream. Sometimes they would have a band play there on Friday nights. Lots of folks showed up for the treats, the good music and just to meet up with other folks.

Sometimes I would go uphill to a friend's house. I had to work hard to get my bike up the hill, but coming home was like flying. This family was real poor, but their mom was a sweet lady. She worked real hard keeping her five kids and the house. Their dad treated them all mean though, and he drank a lot. I learned not to come by when he was home.

One day, all of the kids went down to the lake behind the house to fish. I left my shoes on the porch because I didn't want to get them dirty. A neighbor boy who always gave me a hard time filled my shoes with chicken poop. When I came back and found my shoes full of that slimy mess, I started to cry.

When my mom saw, she got in her car. She had a few beers in her then too. She went to his house and barged right in, yelling, "Where is he, your son did this to my daughter?"

I was so embarrassed, plus it only made things worse for me. Every time he saw me riding by on my bike, he would throw rotten apples at me.

He wasn't a very good thrower though; he always missed, and I was good at riding my bike. I would dodge and ride real fast; I think I was better than any boy in my neighborhood.

A neighbor's mom took us all to the movies once. It was the first time I went to a real sit-down movie theater. It was some Disney movie, but I didn't care for it much. I would much rather be outside riding my bike or mowing the yard or climbing trees. I was such a tomboy.

One day, a man came by and picked up the goats. I was sort of glad because the boys on the school bus would always make goat sounds out the window. It made me feel bad, them making fun of our goats, but my brother always said, "Don't pay them any mind. They're just stupid."

Now my brothers were supposed to mow the yard, but I wanted to do it so they let me. I would hang a milk jar from my handlebars and go buy some gas for 25¢. Since my brothers were supposed to be doing this, and since I didn't want them to get in trouble, I would start after dad left for work.

When he got home, he would always ask who mowed the yard and where were my brothers.

I would tell him they were down playing in the creek, swinging on a big rope. I wasn't allowed to go there, but I would anyway. It was a big creek with a waterfall, and water rushed over the rocks. There was a huge log across the creek, big enough to walk on, but I would sit and scoot across.

Once on the other side, I'd go looking for my brothers. They were usually wrestling and playing in a big mud hole, swinging and having lots of fun. They would be covered with mud from top to bottom. Since dad was always asking where they were when he got home, I took to going there shortly before he was due. I would let them know it was about time.

My dad told me never to go to that creek without him along with, but I never told him. Sometimes he would take me there after dinner. He'd carry his shotgun and shoot snakes. He'd point at them and say, "That's why I don't want you kids in the creek." But we were kids and didn't listen.

One day after school, my brothers went to play in the woods. Later my sister and I heard a knock on the door. It was my oldest brother. He was very upset and asked my sister if he could come in. It was real strange, him knocking and asking to come into his own home. He was real scared though; my other brother had climbed up high in a pine tree and he had cut the tree out from under him. A neighbor had taken him to the hospital; his arm was broken.

When my dad found out, they went and saw the tree. Dad didn't spank my brother, but there was a real long talking to going on. Since my brother's arm and shoulder were broken up, he couldn't sleep in a bed, so dad had to buy a recliner for him to sleep in. I would bring his homework from school. I would do it for him too, most of the time, and take it back to the teacher the next day. He passed too; I was smarter than I thought.

I was also the mail girl. All the girls would send him love letters and notes, drawing hearts on them. It made my brother happy so I didn't complain; I missed him not being on the bus with me.

For fifth grade, I had Mrs. S___. My grades were always average to okay, never really great, but never bad. What I liked best about school was going outside and playing; I looked forward to break time, playing kick ball and swinging on the swings.

My brothers would sometimes have their friends over to play football in our back yard. I loved to watch, sitting on the sidelines. My brothers would sometimes play with me and they taught me how to throw; they always said I was pretty good. One day, when they were short a player, my brother said, "Al can play."

The other boys didn't believe it; I was just a little girl, though I was eleven now. My brother brought me in on his side and they found out real fast how good I could play. I could run fast and I could catch a pass. Best of all, I could throw one too, straight to who I wanted it to go to. Later they all would fuss about whose team I would play on. Of course, I always chose my brothers' team. It was the Walls against the Balls brothers.

There was a lake not far from our house and dad would sometimes take me there to go pole fishing. He always said not to go there alone. I did some anyway, with friends, but I knew it was a very deep lake so I knew to be careful. I would watch out for the other kids too.

One winter day the lake was covered with ice, but the ice wasn't very thick. I saw a boy out on the ice, and I knew he would go down if the ice broke. It did, so I ran fast to a neighbor. He threw a long rope in and brought the boy out of that cold water. He made him smell something and it made the boy throw up the water he'd inhaled. When I told dad about it, he said I did real good getting that boy help.

I can't remember my sixth grade teacher's name, but I graduated. That summer we went to Myrtle Beach and Aunt Sally went with us. Aunt Sally and I laid out on the beach. She kept saying how good the sun felt, but her skin was so fair, the sun fried her.

My dad said to her, "You are going to be burning later." And for sure she was. We had to come home early; she blistered so badly all over. All she could stand was just a bed sheet draped around her. I felt so bad for her. We didn't have air conditioning, but we had to keep the car windows rolled up so the hot air didn't blow on her. No one could touch her, because she hurt so badly.

We spent a lot of time that summer swimming at the Crystal Lake pool. My brothers would jump off the high dive and show off for the girls. In another building, you could go upstairs and put a quarter in their jukebox and dance to the music. There was a snack bar there too where you could get hotdogs, burgers, and sodas. I went some, but mostly I stayed home to watch my little brother and help mom with the house and yard chores.

The favorite trick my oldest brother liked to play on me was when we were crossing the Yadkinville River Bridge, he'd tell me the bridge is falling. It is such a long bridge; what he said would scare me. I still have those thoughts when crossing that river bridge.

Seventh grade was a big deal; I was in junior high school now and it was a new school, Northwest Junior High. A new school meant making new friends and going to new classes. I loved my PE teacher, but then I loved playing sports and working out and feeling good about myself.

Junior high was different. We went to seven different classes during the day instead of staying in one room being taught by one teacher. Every class had a different teacher, but this is when you start growing up and getting prepared for high school. My grades were average to above average, but I got a lot of 'needs to improve on conduct'—I talked too much in class.

My brother brought a car home one day. It was a red Ford Falcon. He was only fifteen, so I think someone gave it to him. It had a bad starter that didn't work more often than it did. When the key didn't work, it was my job to start it rolling down that driveway so he could pop the clutch and get it started. I was only ninety-five pounds then; it was hard for me to push that car, but he'd offer to take me for a ride for all my hard work. Sometimes I'd go. I didn't mind helping my brother; he was always good to me. He ended up selling that car and making a little money.

My brothers had grown up handsome, and girls at school were always wanting to be my friend so they could come to my house just to see them or meet them. I caught on quick and paid those girls no mind. Of course I told my brothers all about it.

I was in the eighth grade when we moved to a new home off Cherry Street in Winston Salem. The old place was getting too run down. The hardwood floors needed to be replaced; they creaked badly when I walked across them. If my baby brother was sleeping, I had to be quick moving across the floor. At night, the sound was real scary. There were cracks in the walls too, so we moved across town to a housing project and new friends everywhere; I missed all my old friends though.

The new place was in a housing development. Our address was 100 Cherryview Lane. Being a housing development meant that the government owned our home and my folks paid the house payment to the Housing Authority of Winston Salem. All the homes in our neighborhood looked the same, and they were so close together. I missed the big yard.

My oldest brother was eighteen and drove a car. He would pick me up for the last two months of my eighth year. He was already picking up his girl. She would eventually become my sister-in-law. I love her a lot.

The development was brand new and it was spring when we moved there. They'd just seeded in the new grass and it was getting almost tall enough to mow. Dad told me not to mow the grass, but I decided to do it anyway. All of a sudden I hear a big noise under the mower and then the blade came off and hit the frame, and a piece of the frame hit me in the side of my leg. I pulled the piece of metal out, and when I looked up the nice lady who lived next door was there, telling me to turn the mower off, but it went dead.

She ran and got my oldest brother. He was sleeping because he worked third shift. He took me to the hospital in his new red car. He drove so fast getting me there, though I wasn't bleeding much. Mom wasn't home so they called dad. I was scared thinking what my dad would say when he came. I was sure I was going to be in hot water.

By the time he arrived they had numbed me up pretty good. Dad pulled the curtain back and the look on his face wasn't what I expected. His mouth was open. "Are you okay?"

I was upset and scared. "Yes sir."

"I told you, Allison Dawn, *not* to mow the yard."

"I know."

He stayed and took me home. We talked all the way home. He wasn't as upset as I thought he would be, but I learned not to mow unless I was certain there were no rocks or other things left over from building a house. That summer wasn't much fun for a while, but I was soon mowing with a new mower. I wore jeans and boots from then on though.

I started ninth grade at Atkins High school and stayed there for tenth grade too. It was clear across town. This was when white kids were bussed to black schools and black kids were bussed to white schools. Going all the way across town never made any sense to me, but I liked the school all right.

Sometimes a friend of my brother's would take me to and from school; he worked at Reynolds Tobacco Company, and the school was along the way, so him picking me up was easy. Sometimes he'd take me to get a snack like ice cream or a soda. He also taught me how to play tennis.

I was asked out by a lot of guys in school, but I was too shy and never went out. Plus, with my folks always drinking and fighting, I didn't want anyone to come over. My brother's friend was four years older than I was, and he'd been a friend a long time, so him coming over was okay. He would sometimes take me to his place to give me a break from my family and my little brother. I discovered him with another girl one day when he was supposed to have been meeting me. I was so jealous; I ended our relationship right there.

There were several nice guys in my homeroom. One would meet me at my locker right after homeroom. He'd look me right in the eyes; he had such pretty green eyes. He asked me to go steady with him; he was in really good shape—very nice looking. Me knowing how things were at home, I said I'd think about it. The next day, I decided I had to tell him no. I tried to be nice about it, but I guess he thought I shot him down. Later I found out he was the most valuable player in his last school, and he got it both years at this school. He went on to play football at North Forsyth High and in college. He came from a real church-going family and would have been a good pick—I missed out on that one.

The Dixie Classic Fair came to town on the first of October. I met a guy there and we rode rides; he won lots of stuffed animals for me by playing basketball. I liked to watch him play and I let him give some of the toys to my girlfriends. I thought he shot better than a pro; it was lots of fun. I only saw him at school sometimes; he was a year ahead of me. He lived with his grandmother. Later I found out that his parents were divorced.

One day, he rode his bicycle all the way to my house in the pouring rain. When he knocked on the door my brother answered. When my brother came to get me, I told him to tell the guy I wasn't home. I felt bad thinking how far he'd come, and in the rain.

The football coach was my math teacher, and one day he called me to stay after class. I was kind of scared. What had I done to be held after class? All he said was that all the football players thought I was pretty enough and smart enough to be on the Home Coming Court, but I couldn't; I wasn't a junior. That's all he had to tell me. That the football team thought I was pretty. I said, "Thank you," and scooted out of that room fast. Aside from feeling really embarrassed about being held after class, it made me feel good about myself.

That summer, I started watching my sister's kids. I was always looking for some kind of work so I could help my parents by buying as much of my own things as I could.

Our deal was $20 and a new dress a week. For that I took care of her kids, a six-month old boy, a girl who was about a year and a half, and a boy who was around three, and their home. I did things like washing the clothes and seeing that they were folded and put away; ironing if needed. I even started dinner for them. She always said I was a big help. I learned a lot about managing a home with kids under foot, but I would go home Friday evenings and go back on Sunday evenings; it gave me a break.

She made me eight dresses and I bought a pair of baby doll shoes to wear with them.

I got my driver's license that fall so my dad took me to get my first car. It was a Dodge Dart, three speed on the column. He said before he bought it, "You have a car now, it's up to you to get a job and pay for the insurance and buy your own gas. There will be no speeding and no staying out late. You still have school to finish."

I got a job at Hardee's Fast Food that summer and worked the cash register. When school started back up, I worked part time after school and on weekends. I made $1.65 an hour. I made enough for gas and car insurance, and had extra to buy clothes.

I really liked my little Dart; it could fly. But after paying for two speeding tickets, I had to learn how to put my need for speed on a diet. I had insurance and gas to buy; I didn't need to be paying for speeding tickets too. When I told my dad, he just said, "You should have known better." Well, I sure do now. My speeding tickets caused my insurance bill to go up.

For my junior and senior high school years, I went to North Forsyth Senior High. I loved this school; there was always lots of things going on. It was also a lot closer to home, being only a five-minute drive. I went to school from seven thirty in the morning until eleven. I would come directly home after school, do my homework and then go to work at a factory named CLR Manufacturing. They made paper tubes for yarn to be put on. My job was a packer. I stood along with others and took these tubes off the line and packed them in a huge box. I had to inspect them as well, to make sure they were made good. I worked from three in the afternoon until eleven at night. This was real grown-up work. Not at all like working at a fast food place. I was expected to put in a full forty-hour week.

During my senior year, a nice black girl came and knocked on our door. She lived just up the street from me and she could sing out of this world. I let her ride with me to school.

There were only three white families in our neighborhood so I learned to like all races.

Mom didn't work after we moved to 100 Cherryview Lane. She had to take my little brother clear across town to his school and to his many doctors' appointments.

Mom got sick once and had to spend a few days in the hospital. When she came home, dad started fussing at her and got her all upset. I had seen and heard enough so I stepped in between them.

My dad told me to move, but I wouldn't so we ended up having a big argument.

I left and moved in with my girlfriend's parents. They had a good home and didn't mind if I stayed. My girlfriend and I ended up getting an apartment. It was fun for a while, but then someone broke into our place and stole lots of things. They took my bike and my jewels and some clothes. My girlfriend had just gone shopping for new clothes. We were scared so we moved back to her home.

I was only gone from home for around two months, but my dad was very upset. He came by and he started to cry. I learned how bad he felt about what happened and my being gone.

After I moved back home, I learned very fast not to go back out after getting home from work unless he knew where I was and with who.

I came home at six in the morning one time and dad was there at the door. "What are you doing outside?" he asked.

At first I was going to say I was getting the newspaper, then I started to say something else.

My dad said, "We will talk when I get home from work."

I wasn't there when he got home; I'd gone to work, but later he laid down the law to me.

I graduated from high school on the 5th of June 1975. I remember my oldest brother and his wife came home from Germany, and they attended the graduation ceremony. My class was the largest class to graduate; six hundred students were to walk across the stage. The ceremony was held at the Coliseum in Winston Salem. Being named Walls meant I was almost the last person to make that walk, but as I started to leave the stage, I heard my brother's special whistle. I was so happy.

Chapter 3

After graduation, my best girlfriend and I drove to Myrtle Beach. We had booked a room to stay for only a week, but ended up staying two. My girlfriend hung out with her boyfriend most of the time. I didn't have a boyfriend; I hung out with my brother and other friends. I had such a good time; it was hard going back home again. My parents had always said they would get a divorce as soon as I graduated, and they never changed that, even after my little brother was born.

Mom and dad separated soon after I got back. I don't know what was happening with my sister, but she got her divorce about then too. She asked me to move into an apartment with her to help with the rent. It was a brand new apartment complex over in Stanleyville. The complex was called Willow Creek Apartments. We lived in apartment 34B; I remember that because it sounded like a bra size. I'd never lived in an apartment before; they were all alike. It was an okay place. It had two bedrooms upstairs and a little deck off the back. I hadn't lived with my sister for a long time, not since she'd gotten married nine years ago.

Her three kids would come stay with us every other weekend; it was hard for her being a mom and missing her kids, but her and her husband had agreed that it would be better for them to live with him. He had the better paying job and the home they had built together. It was sad, but we kept busy working and doing things together sometimes.

She had a boyfriend, but that didn't last long. She liked to criticize whoever I dated, always making bad comments about how they looked or what they wore or where they took me. I guess the difference was her growing up in the sixties and me growing up in the seventies. Things change in ten years.

Now that all us kids had pretty much scattered across town with homes of our own, and even families, we would get together for holidays and birthdays, but two years after mom and dad separated, their divorce was finalized. It was an ugly affair; my sister, my youngest brother, and I ended up going to court for a judge to decide who my youngest brother would stay with because my mom had a bad drinking problem by then. My brother ended up staying with dad, and mom left. None of us heard from her for twelve years; we didn't even know where she went.

One day while at work, I started to feel bad, I felt so unusually tired so I went to see the nurse at work. She started poking around and asking questions the way nurses will do, and while she was checking under my jaw, she discovered a lump. She told me it was in my thyroid gland and that it needed to be removed right away. I remembered then that my grandmother had something like this years ago. With everything that was going on, the last thing I wanted to do was create another bill, but I would certainly be no help if I got worse. The doctor told me these things could be caused by stress and not resting. Well, I suppose that certainly applies. The surgery went well though. They removed half of my thyroid gland along with a non-cancerous tumor.

I was only in the hospital for a few days. My dad and my sister made sure everything was taken care of while I was there. When I got home, we were in the new place so it was better for me to rest. In no time I was back to work. The hardest part about the whole thing was that my mom wasn't there and no one knew where she was.

Dad and my brother lived next door to his sister. She was a good lady and a hard worker. Dad did a good job raising my brother, but mom just leaving us all like that still hurt.

I guess the hardest part for me was the ladies at work would be planning things with their mothers and talking about things they'd done during the holidays. If they were talking about their mother, I tried not to listen. I worked hard to block them out; it hurt so much.

I know it hurt the rest of the family too. My sister and I would talk about it once in a while.

Mom and dad might not have been able to live together peacefully, but he still worried about her. I hated it when he'd ask me if I'd heard from her. Telling my dad no and seeing the hurt was the worst. They'd been married for thirty years.

For my twenty-first birthday, my sister and I threw a big party on Saturday night. We sent out about fifty invitations to lots of my friends, they all showed up at the Club House with their dates. The place was packed tight; they opened the doors and rows of friends came in. Some of the family came too, and everyone brought their own bottles of whatever, everything. I gave all the beer to the band. They played rock and roll, bluegrass, and seventies stuff; they were the greatest. I had lots of cake and too much to drink, and ended up missing some of my own party, but the others rocked on until at least two in the morning.

The last thing I remember was a very good friend asking me how it felt being a grown woman.

It was our party so we were responsible for the cleanup; I woke up to a clean club; there were lots of trash bags full of beer cans and bottles. I found out that my sister had made her special friend bag everything up.

My sister and I got along fairly well, I thought. I worked and she worked, and we would or wouldn't have our nightlife as the mood moved us. I liked to go to the Casablanca Club. I'd meet some of my girlfriends there and we'd listen to rock and roll. There was also a nice pool and a tennis court at our complex where we could spend a sunny afternoon.

My sister and I always went shopping together for food. We didn't have lots of money so we ate lots of tomato soup. My sister to this day hates tomato soup. She did the cooking when her kids were there for their weekend stay.

We had a little black poodle named Bow while we lived there. He decided to eat the zipper out of my boots one day while I was taking a nap. My sister came rushing in wanting to go grocery shopping so I scooped up my boots and went to zip them up, only there was no zipper. Oh, was I so angry at that dog. I got over it though; he was a mess, but I loved that dog.

My sister and I moved from the Willow Creek Apartments to an older type of rent house a friend of hers told us about. My sister started hanging out with this fat guy who walked with a cane. I never liked him, but I never said as much. He always gave me the creeps; he always had a grin on his face like he knew something that others didn't. Every time he came around, I would find an excuse to go somewhere else.

One October day I came home from work. I was planning to go out with a girlfriend, but I needed to change. This creepy fat guy was sitting at the kitchen table. He'd brought us a cherry pie his mother made for us. I'm not sure why he brought a cherry pie, saying it was for us, when my sister doesn't eat cherries. It looked really good though. He called it Cherry Yum Yum; just looking at it, confirmed the name, but I was going out and in a bit of a hurry to get ready; a girlfriend of mine was coming to pick me up. As I walked past where he was sitting, out of the blue, he said, "Allison, how would it feel having lizards crawling all over you?" He stretched out his arms across the table and had this self-satisfied smirk on his face.

I stopped and just looked at him. It struck me as incredibly strange. Why would anyone say such a thing?

When my girlfriend came, I told her about him and what he'd said. She agreed with me; the guy was weird. She said, "I don't understand why your sister is letting him come into your home."

When I went to the bathroom to get ready, he told her that he could tell things like the unknown. She told me about it on the way to the Casablanca Club. It was good to rock the night away, and get far away from the strange people my sister chose to spend her time with.

When I got home from the club, I had a pleasant buzz going and there was that pie, calling my name, looking so yummy with brown sugar sprinkled on top. I couldn't resist; my sister wasn't going to eat any and it would be a shame for it to go to waste, so I cut myself a slice and dug in. A small bit of sweet cherry heaven before I went to bed.

I woke the next morning with the worst headache I'd ever had in my life; I couldn't move. It felt like my head was going to pop right off my shoulders. My throat swelled up and I was running a fever; I felt chilled for days. Every time I tried to eat, I wanted to throw up, but if I didn't, in no time at all it would come out the other end; I was so sick, all I could do was lay there.

My sister would come and go from work like I was just another piece of furniture. She never offered to bring me any food or drink, not that I could eat or drink anything. She never offered to take me to the doctor, not that I had any way to pay them; I didn't have money for a doctor and I didn't have insurance from my work. She'd just stick her head in as if to see if I was still alive. She could see me lying there shaking and sweating. She didn't even offer to bring me any Tylenol for the pain.

I'd somehow manage to make it to the shower every day, but I felt like I was going to pass out doing it. I felt like I was drying up like a prune, so I would go stand in the shower for a little while. Then I would put lotion on my body; my skin soaked it up like a dry sponge. I saw myself in the mirror one day and what I saw scared me. I had a nice tan, but my skin was gray and the whites of my eyes were yellow and bloodshot.

I called Aunt Sally and asked her to pray with me. It felt like a hammer was banging around inside my head; I couldn't even touch the top of my head, I hurt so bad.

I remember one day; my sister had gone over to Fat Boy's place. I can't remember why, but for some reason I called her there. She thought it was so funny; you see, she told me that her and Fat Boy were in their minds seeing me dial the phone and watching it ring, watching themselves pick it up. She said it was this energy that made me call them, that it was mind over matter. Was I so sick that I was hallucinating? I suppose that is a possibility, but I don't think I was *that* sick. I have a very good memory and I can remember every day of this torture, and that really freaked me out.

It took about a week before I could make it to the bathroom without my head exploding. It was the worst week of my life, but, thank God, I recovered and I was soon back to work.

About a month later, I came home after work to find Fat Boy helping my sister move out. I had no idea what was going on. She had never mentioned anything about moving. I was pretty upset; I tried to rent the place myself, but it was already promised to someone else; they were waiting. My dad was upset about it too. Unfortunately, his place was way too small, and since the power had already been turned off, it was too cold to stay where I was. Dad loaned me enough money to rent a hotel room for a week until I could move my things out and find somewhere else to live.

One day I ran into my brother's friend. He told me he lived with his sister and a girlfriend of hers; they all rented an older home and they needed another roommate so I moved in with them. The girls were a mess. They smoked pot and acted silly. I didn't care to be around them much.

I had a little Dachshund dog I named Snoopy, I called him Snoot, and I'd take him out for a ride. I had a tan Volkswagen then, and he would sit on my lap and look out the window; he liked the air blowing in his face. I loved that dog.

I didn't like living there. The girls would trash the kitchen and bathroom, and there was really no private place, but the rent was cheap. One day I was sitting in the living room and one of the girls threw an umbrella at Snoopy from the top of the stairs. I went *off!* I yelled at them, "You just wait a minute."

They came down laughing, thinking it was funny.

I put Snoopy in my room and I followed them out as they got into a car. I started to give them a piece of my mind, and it wasn't a nice piece. As I was yelling at them, my boyfriend drove up. He pulled me away and told me to stop before I got any more heated up. I left to cool down for a bit, but when I got back I discovered that my roommates had thrown a full-sized mattress on top of my twin bed. I was fed up.

I started packing my things to move in with my boyfriend when the sister I hadn't heard from for eight months, not since she just up and moved out on me, calls me up and asks me to come over. I told her I was in the process of moving in with my boyfriend, and that I would call back once I was settled. I took down her new number and continued with my move.

My boyfriend and I knew a guy who owned an older home near the Yadkinville River, and he let us rent a bedroom. I put my furniture in storage while we looked for a better place. I felt safe living there; several of my other friends knew him. It was peaceful there.

I got tired of folding pantyhose at the Hanes Manufactory. I worked on piecework, folding pantyhose, placing them to be dyed. I thought there had to be a better way to make a living so I gave it up. I got paid by the piece, and it was real hard to make a good weekly paycheck. I enrolled for a clerical class in the local college to improve my chances of getting a better job later, and I got a job at

Biscuit Ville working from six in the morning until two in the afternoon running the cash register and making ham biscuits for the guests. It wasn't the greatest job, but it was a job. It was a long drive, but the owners were very nice people and I liked the early hours.

My sister worked at the Olds Dealership in the office. It was a good job and she made much better money than I did, but she never came up to buy lunch at Biscuit Ville.

Her being so close, I decided to return her call. I dug the number out and thought long and hard about it. She lived in Old Town and she invited me to come over. Going to visit her was strange, and she had changed. She'd never had a lot of natural color in her skin before, but now she'd bleached her hair blond and she had a tan. I thought it made her look like an over-aged beach bum, but it was her hair so I didn't say anything.

Her apartment building was a long, one-story building and she told me about how much she loved it there. She knew all her neighbors; they were all single ladies and they would get together for meals and good times. My sister and her next-door neighbor would go out to adult bars and go dancing sometimes.

I asked her how she found the place, and she told me how her creepy fat friend knew the area and he'd helped her find the place. I didn't really need the reminder about that guy, but I had to ask after him; it was the polite thing to do.

She chatted along about how she'd taken him to the beach with her and the kids for a week after they got out of school. She knew his mom. She kept saying they were just friends. I kept thinking he was a pretty strange friend, especially since I'd once heard him refer to her as his sister – the thought made me shudder.

She went on to tell me how she had taken a class on how to read Tarot cards. She told me the other ladies she'd taken the class with were the upper crust of the community; it sounded like she was bragging about rubbing shoulders with high society.

I had never heard of tarot before, so she got her cards out to show me. She thought they were pretty and said as much as she pointed out all the different things or people on the cards. She said there were all different kinds of decks, but that she had bought hers and a book from her class.

While I was there, one of her neighbors dropped by. My sister introduced me to her, and right off the neighbor said, "Well, you two don't look like sisters."

My sister's best saying for that was, "She got the looks and I got the brains."

I really hated that saying, always have, and always will. I told her that my mom was tall and my dad is short. But I thought, *Why didn't my sister tell anyone that we didn't have the same father? She sure didn't mind telling me in front of her kids how she hated me for being small and how I was a spoiled brat, and about when I got a baby doll one Christmas and all she got was a diary and a scarf.* I never understood that picture. Was it to make her friends think I had no brains, that I was just a dizzy, sandy-haired, girl ten years younger than her?

When the woman left, we went back to talking about her cards and her classes. By the time I left, she promised to give me a reading. I had never heard of a reading, though I figured from the way she talked that it had something to do with her fancy cards.

When I got home, I told my boyfriend's sister about it and she got a reading, then a male friend of my boyfriend went and got one. They said she knew things and told them things, and that there was no way she could have known. I thought, *Okay, we'll see about this.* I called my sister and asked if I could get a reading with her Tarot cards.

When I got there, she placed a crystal bowl full of salt water on the table, and then got her cards out. She shuffled them, and then handed them to me to cut into three parts and restack. When I handed them back, she started to lay them out, telling me the meanings of each card as she went. It was interesting, but it gave me the willies; I didn't care for her knowing my business or giving me details of my past or future.

When she was done, she started telling me about how a boyfriend she'd met through her creepy fat friend was moving down from New Jersey. She told me that she'd done quite a few tarot readings up there. I thought, *She is really into this to go that far and stay up all night to read cards with funny looking pictures on them all weekend whenever she didn't have her kids over, and then come back and go to work on Monday.*

Then I thought back to when we were kids. My mom would sometimes bring out a regular deck of playing cards. She read them once for my sister and told her she would one day get a divorce. That had come true. Maybe there was something to these cards.

I went home and talked with my boyfriend about this puzzle. He was a nice, respectful guy, he never had a lot to say, but he was a good listener. I don't think he favored my sister. Whenever he talked about her, he'd only say good things, but the list was pretty short so he didn't say much at all. He was a few years older than I was so I felt that his advice was pretty solid; he was a good judge of people.

My sister called me one day and said there was a job at Old Town Towel Shop in sales so I applied and got the job making a dollar more per hour, much better for me. I soon learned how my sister had found out about the job. I was working with her fat friend's mother. She was real nice and we became good friends. The owner was a nice lady who lived in my old neighborhood over near Speas Road; she came by in the afternoons. We sold towels, comforters, bedspreads, racks to hang things on, and shower curtains to ladies who wanted to decorate their homes with different colors and good brand names.

I got to know Fat Boy's mom pretty well. She told me all about how he never got a job and would just lay around down in her basement doing nothing while she did all the work. She told me how my sister came by often and would take him to the YMCA to work out and spend time together. Most of the time she would just come and they would talk, though she didn't know what about.

My sister took me there once; he sat on a king-size bed with a big grin on his face the entire time. He kept saying how my sister and I didn't look anything alike. He laughed like a little kid who didn't know what else to say or do. Then he insisted on taking my sister's ring. He said he could tell her future by reading the vibes. I thought, *How silly is this guy?*

I got uncomfortable there, especially when he offered us something to drink. We said no and left. Later, my sister told me that he was such a nice person and that he had been in some kind of bad wreck and was laid up. To me, he just looked fat and lazy, using his mom for what he needed.

Since I was working in Old Town now, I found an upstairs apartment in a nearby complex, which was closer to work. I worked at the Towel Shop for about two years, until I found a better paying job. The job I found was at the Medical Park Pharmacy where I worked with the owner. I would run drugs to the doctors in the Park and all across the city. I even took deposits to the bank when asked. The pay was a little better, but the hours were a lot better, and I never had to work weekends.

Things had turned around for my sister, but it didn't last long. Her new boyfriend she'd met in New Jersey had moved in with her and then he'd got a good job at Reynolds Tobacco Company. But they weren't getting along so well. He'd bring a guy friend of his over and they'd leave beer cans stacked all over the place, so she moved out on him. I saw them together once; they looked like mother and son, the age difference was so visible. She ended up moving into the apartment right under mine. Whenever I saw her, she seemed depressed, but she still carried on, and her kids still came over every other weekend. I felt sorry for her, a little, but as the saying goes, what goes around, comes around. I hadn't forgotten how she had moved out on me and left me with no place to go.

My sister and I didn't have the same friends anymore and I was now working at the bank. I had gone in one day and they asked me if I wanted to apply, so I did and got the job. I was a teller now, working most of the time at the drive-through; I liked being back there alone. I was still shy, and I certainly didn't want to be on the front teller line. It was a super job, and the ladies who worked there were wonderful. I had learned a lot from them, but I wasn't sleeping well, which made me feel jumpy and hyper, restless even.

When they promoted me to front teller, I didn't like it, so I gave my notice and got a job at Winston Salem Health Care Plan as a medical records clerk. The job wasn't full time to start, but I worked hard and soon moved up to a full time position with benefits.

While I worked there, I made friends with a lady who needed to move closer. She drove thirty minutes to and from work every day. She was going through a rough time with her little girl. I told her I would be willing to get a two-bedroom apartment with her and we could share expenses. She was so happy with the idea, so I moved to the other end of my complex and she moved in with her four-year-old daughter. We didn't work in the same department, but she was a good roommate and a good mother and became a life-long friend.

I worked second shift so I would work out in the morning. My sister still lived in the same complex, but we hardly ever spoke. I'd think about how we used to be though, often. I never could understand why she had treated me so different after meeting Fat Boy. My dad would say, "Why is she hanging out with him so often?" I never brought it up though. She was my big sister and I respected her, and I didn't want to start the same argument all over again. I wondered if God was trying to show me something, or was I a lesson for her?

We are as different from me as can be. She was tall and kept her hair short. She was controlling and outspoken. It was 'her first' or 'nothing'. I was short, pretty, and painfully shy until I got to know you. And yet I could see jealousy rolling off her every time we met. I didn't agree with her favorite saying of, 'she got the looks but I got the brains', but I kept my mouth shut, I just wanted to love her as my sister and not get any more bitter over something that had happened in the past.

I poured all my restless and hyper energy into my work and was eventually able to buy a house. It was a three-bedroom house with a deck off the back.

One night I was going to meet some of my girlfriends at a place over on Thirty Street called Muddy Duck. A cop car pulled up next to me as I was parking. The cop shined his big flashlight in my car and then says, "I've been looking for you."

I thought, *Who is this, and why me?*

It turns out he and I went to North Forsyth High School together. He asked if he could give me a call sometime. I remembered him so I said yes.

About a week later this old time high school friend who was now a police officer with the Winston Salem Police Department called and asked me out on a date. He took me to a nice restaurant and we caught up. Mind you, I was nervous all the time these days so I didn't talk much. He told me all about his two little boys.

He and I worked the same shift and his Honda would break down all the time, so sometimes he would call me at work and ask for a ride home.

I started to really like him, and his boys. They were so sweet, and always fun. I would watch them sometimes when he would go on a moonlight job.

After I got my house, I signed my apartment lease over to my roommate. He and his brother were kind enough to move me into my new house one night while I was at work. His whole family was so sweet.

I will never forget taking my dad to see it for the first time. As we were driving along, he said, "Dang, Allison, how much farther?"

I just laughed and said, "Not much." He was so proud of me being able to buy a house all by myself.

I was still having trouble sleeping, and my hyper nervousness was only getting worse. It was like someone was winding me up like a spring. Everything I did was fast. I talked fast. I worked fast. That wouldn't be so bad if I could sleep, but it seemed like I could never wind down.

Over time my cop boyfriend and I grew apart and went our separate ways. I still miss him at times, but he wasn't ready to settle down and I was too nervous.

Sometime later a cousin of mine wanted to introduce me to one of his high school buddies. This guy was tall, nice looking, and had a two-year-old boy. His wife had gotten sick and passed away. He worked with wood, and he took me on a trip to Florida to a friend's house to see a bed he'd made for them. Then he took me to Disney World. It was a whirlwind weekend, and we had lots of fun, but I really wasn't into it. I knew it was just me and my being hyper all the time. He told me he wanted to marry me and that he would give me a good life. He promised to build me a swimming pool in the back yard. He was a hard worker and had his own home in Clemmons in a good neighborhood. He was very nice and his little boy was so cute, but I just couldn't agree. I was so confused and hyper all the time, so I ended our relationship one day when he came to see me at work.

I ended up going to the doctor because I was getting so ragged and yet couldn't seem to stop. He wrote me a prescription for ten milligrams of Ativan for anxiety.

I missed my mom. Maybe being sick made it worse, but still no one had heard a peep from her. I just kept praying she would return one day.

I kept things going though. I even got a part time job on the weekends, but I still felt terrible. I felt incredibly tired all the time, but my being so hyper just wouldn't let me slow down. I'd take some Ativan and then I was zonked out and have to lay my head down on my desk. I just wanted to pass out then. When the pill wore off, I was back to being tired but wound up hyper again; there was no middle ground.

I would talk to my dad, often, and he'd listen patiently as I told him about all the things that were going wrong in my life. One day he asked me, "Allison, are you on drugs?"

It broke my heart that he would ask me such a question, but he was my father so I answered him truthfully. "No, I'm not on drugs. Why would you ask me if I'm taking drugs?"

Dad said, "Allison, you are so hard and unkind. Not only to yourself, but to others. Every time I talk to you it's bad news."

My dad was right. I was hard on everyone around me. But this wasn't me; none of this was the person I was raised to be, the person I had been all of my life until things started to go wrong.

I went back to the doctor and had him test me for drugs; it came back negative. While I was there, I explained the feeling I was having in my lower back, how it felt like something was moving inside of me there. He sent me for an x-ray, but nothing showed up.

I told him how my mind wouldn't slow down, ever, unless I took the medicine and then it made me too sleepy to work. When he didn't have anything else to say, I just got in my car and left. I took the drug test to show my dad so he wouldn't worry.

Chapter 4

I couldn't sit at a desk anymore so I quit my job and went to cosmetology school to learn how to cut hair. Then I sold my house and moved back to Old Town.

My youngest brother was married now and had a baby girl in December of 1985. Our family still got together for holidays. Life was good for the rest of my family, but I was changing jobs right and left, and I was so hyper my hands were shaking.

My sister and I hardly spoke at all. She had met someone else and had moved into a house over in Rural Hall. She still had the same job and her kids were growing up. Whenever I saw her, she was her usual bossy self.

Somehow I made it each month, paying my bills and such. It was hard keeping myself going, wondering what was making me feel so bad and act so different. I swear I could feel something moving around in my lower back. Anymore I felt like I was being forced to do everything fast. I wasn't just wound up and nervous, I was the Roadrunner on Speed, and when I got to talking, it came out like a record playing too fast, it was near babbling. Even my perception was changing, drastically. I had no time for anyone, and irrational fears were creeping in around the edges.

Cosmetology school was not at all what I expected. All these older ladies came in to get their hair done cheap and left no tips. Nearly all of them wanted their gray hair dyed blue or red. The blue I can understand, it was the fashion, but the red... How many redheads do you see at that age? True redheads? Not many, but we sure turned out our fair share.

One Saturday morning my instructor called me up to the front of the class to do a cut on a client, but it wasn't another little old lady, it was a good looking man wanting a shampoo and a trim and I was supposed to do it in front of the whole class.

After I finished, he tipped me well and my instructor said it was an excellent cut. I guess ladies aren't for me. I decided right there that I needed to go to barbering college.

Barbering college was so different, it was the most laid back place I had ever attended. There were more men attending, but best of all, no more blue heads to worry about.

The place had two rows of barber chairs; the girls were on one side and the guys had the other side. Clients would come for a shampoo and cut, or a beard trim and shave. I had a great director; he took a liking to me and put me on the guys' side.

There was another girl student there who took a dislike to me even though I tried to be nice to everyone. She would always give me dirty looks and talk bad about me. I always heard about what she was saying though.

One day the director and I went to the tire store up the street to check out the sale they were having. When we got back we were in his office just hanging out and talking about the sale. All of a sudden Ms. Dislike came in and grabbed me by my collar and asked me why I didn't like her.

I said, "Look, I'll give you one second to get your hands off my collar." But I guess she had to learn the hard way. I pushed myself up out of my chair and punched her, hitting her right in the eye.

The director came around the desk, yelling, "Stop! Stop!" I was all ready to give her another lick, but I stopped.

I was so upset; I'd never done anything like that before. I'm sure he had some explaining to do to his wife about why my red lipstick was all over his nice white shirt and tie. Ms. Know-it-all had picked the wrong person to fight with, and in front of the director too; she got expelled.

The next day, all the guys were calling me by the name of every boxer in the profession. I never did live that one down.

One day, I met one of the girls from cosmetology school. She wanted me to move in with her at her parents' house. We didn't have to pay rent, just power, phone, and cable.

The spring of 1987 was just starting to show her colors when I got a phone call from Aunt Sally. She told me she had a visitor who wanted to see me. I was curious, but she refused to tell me who it was so I went to see for myself.

When Aunt Sally answered the door, she had a huge grin on her face. She didn't say anything, she just ushered me in, and who do you think I saw standing there? God had finally answered my prayers. My mom had come back. She was alive and she was safe and she looked healthy. I was so relieved.

As soon as we got past all that, we sat down for a serious talk. I told her how her just vanishing like that had hurt us all really bad. She knew she'd done wrong, but she was very upset and didn't know who to turn to or where to go.

I wanted to know all about what had happened and where she lived now. She told me she lived in Tampa Florida and she had a roommate. He was an older man; they lived together to share the bills. Life had been hard for her, trying to make ends meet, but she didn't drink anymore and she had found the Lord. She told me she had stayed away because she was depressed about not being married to my dad. She loved him very much still, but she needed to get help with her drinking before she would let herself come back into our lives. She could only stay a few days, but she promised to return as often as she could. I was so happy. My mom coming back into my life was a tiny glimmer of happy in the fogged-out chaos of my existence.

The girlfriend I lived with also befriended an older man who was a full time pilot. He was another tiny glimmer of happy. He flew a King Air Carolina Blue turboprop. He and I became friends too. He was trying to get over two other relationships so he enjoyed us just being friends without being romantically involved. He had a lot of dogs at his house. I would go over and take care of them if he was going to be gone too long.

The owners of the seven-seater jet he flew liked to go to the beach for dinner so he would invite me along. They would go their way and he and I would rent a car. He'd take me to a nice restaurant for a seafood dinner. One day he took me for a half-day deep-sea fishing trip. I had so much fun; I caught more fish that day than anyone else on the boat. He tipped a guy to take the fish off my hook. The little redheaded boy caught on fast and then we both were having fun.

I took him to meet my sister one afternoon; that was a mistake. She didn't like him. She looked at us like, 'are you allowed to breathe the same air as me?' She let her smart lip run with her normal rudeness, saying my mom and my brothers had just left; they'd had a cookout. She looked so mad. It wasn't until later that I figured she was probably mad at mom, or mad about her. She and mom never got along well, and my friend and I just happened to arrive in time to catch the backlash of mom's visit. When we left he said, "Boy, you sure don't look or act like your sister."

I knew what he was trying to say. I said, "We don't have the same dad, but I try my best to get along and love her." Us not having the same father should have been the only difference between us, but there was so much more.

To make up for the bad experience with my sister, I took him to meet my dad. They hit it right off. He took us both for a short flight over the piedmont area on a beautiful Sunday morning. I'm not sure that dad had ever been flying before, but he was having fun. Then we started to land in this tiny airport named Walnut Cove Airport. It looked like he was going to tangle into all of the telephone wires, and the runway looked too short. If it all looked bad to me, I wish I could have taken a picture of my dad's face. I asked, "Are you okay?"

He grinned and said, "I'm fine."

In the later part of 1987, shortly before I graduated from Barber College, I moved into my dad's house over in the Bethania area. He lived way back in the woods in a three-bedroom house. It was a pretty place. Other homes were around, but no one was close. We both liked the space; it reminded me of the old place out on Speas road, but he was past planting any kind of a garden and I didn't have the time. My dad, my middle brother, and my younger brother built the home. We all would gather there for Thanksgiving and Christmas Eve dinners. Mom not being there was still a gap in the holidays, but at least we all knew she was fine and could get in touch with her if we wanted. I knew dad missed her especially at these special times.

The last thing before I graduated from barbering college was a hair cutting competition at the Benton Convention Center in Winston Salem. My director asked me if I wanted to enter. I didn't have the entry fee, but my pilot friend paid it for me. I was so keyed up; I wanted to win first place.

He took me shopping for a new dress too so I would look my best. The dress he bought me matched the drape his son would wear as I cut his hair; he had long shiny black hair.

I invited my dad to come, but right before I left, he called saying he'd stepped off his porch wrong and sprang his ankle. I was so disappointed, but he cheered me on and wished me luck.

The contest was held on a Sunday and 200 barbers were there. I was so excited as I took my place and lined up all my tools. There were lots of well-known business owners of shops there and many out of town judges who sold high-dollar products for hair salons like Redken and TRESemmé.

I was so hyper; I couldn't hold my hands still. I thought if I took half an Ativan it would calm me down a little, just so I could get through this competition. I prayed to God to please let me take home a trophy. There were three places that took a trophy and I only wanted one, something to show my dad.

It began and the judges were walking around looking at the head, the tools, the barber, everything. When it was over, and they started calling names, I was holding my breath. They called first place, but it wasn't me. 200 people were at the competition. They called second place, and that wasn't me either. I think my heart was doing jumping jacks. When they called third place and I heard Ms. Allison Dawn Walls, it was very nearly unbelievable. It took me a second or two to realize it was my name they'd called. I went up and got my trophy, and then a long-time barber friend of mine ran up and gave me a big hug. "You won, Allison."

That was a great day. I thanked God for working through my hands and not allowing any mistakes to happen. After the competition, I jumped in my car and took off to a Kentucky Fried Chicken restaurant and bought a big tub of chicken and headed to dad's house for a victory dinner.

When I got there and showed him my trophy, he just smiled and said, "I knew you could do it."

I worked hard and put in all my hours so I could go before the state board and get certified by the State of North Carolina in the spring of 1987.

My pilot friend bought me a plane ticket to Tampa Florida over the Thanksgiving holiday for a graduation gift so I could visit my mom. Mom lived in a very small apartment in a not so good neighborhood, but it was still nice. There were bars over the windows though; I'm not sure what I thought about that. She lived on the first floor; she told me she liked it in case she had to get out during a bad storm or a fire, and her back wasn't good at her age. We had fun talking and catching up. We went shopping for Christmas gifts and enjoyed all the colorful decorations that were already up all over the place. We'd go out to eat some too.

When I got back, I went to work over at Wake Forest Barber Shop. It was okay working there, but I soon went into business with a local owner at her shop called The Deacon's Den. I got the place all cleaned up and then I wanted to hire some of the other students to give us all a chance to make a name for ourselves, but it didn't work that way. The other lady was messy and wasn't interested in helping others. It wasn't long before I pulled my two tanning beds out of The Deacon's Den. I sold my beds and moved into another area.

In April of 1988 I went to work for The Third Generation Barbering Shop in Kernersville. It was a small shop, and if you didn't look close, you would run right past it. But me and the two sisters who owned it were open every morning by 7:30 a.m. and we worked hard until 6:00 p.m. Tuesday through Saturday. It was a lot of hard work; every cut is different, but I got through them. Sometimes my hands would shake and sometimes I had cuts on my fingers, but I never let any of that stop me.

Men talk more than ladies when they're getting their hair cut, or I thought so, but they also tip if you show up regularly and do a good job. I really liked working at that place; it had a history, being passed down for three generations now.

One cool February evening, I was driving down West Mountain Street in Kernersville and I looked to the right. There I saw a big sign with flashing lights in this yard. It read, 'Readings by Zelda'.

Until this moment, I didn't remember, but I'd been here before. I pulled into the driveway and walked up to the house. With my nerves all in a jumble, I rang the bell and a very nice looking lady answered.

"May I help you?"

I was so nervous by now, I could scarcely speak, but I managed to get my question out. "May I see Zelda?"

The nice lady spoke very soft and sweetly. "She passed away some time back. Did you know her?"

I said, "Well, I came here a long time ago. It was when I was around seventeen. Me and three of my friends came here and we all got a reading from Zelda. The lady we saw was very old; she had a long cord running from her pocket that went up to her hearing aid. She blew on the twenty dollars and told us things. All the things she told me came to pass. She spoke of my parents getting a divorce as well as my sister and her husband. She told me I had a brother far away across the big water and he was in Germany, in the Army. Things of that sort, but you said she passed away. I'm sorry to hear that." I turned to leave. But then I remember that Zelda's daughter lived here too with two small children. I turned back and said as much.

The lady smiled such a pretty smile and said, "I have gotten a little older too. If you like, you may come in and get another reading. I do readings as well as my mother did."

"Are you sure?" I said.

She smiled. "I'm sure. Please come in."

I stood there in shock. Another lady, also named Zelda, the daughter of the Zelda I had met, lived in this house and she did readings too.

I entered the house and it was so bright and cheery, just like I remember. There were mirrors all over the walls, from top to bottom. Crystal settings were everywhere. I sat on a soft white sofa and she sat on the matching chair. The leather was like velvet under my hand.

Something about this gentle woman made me pour my life out to her. I told her how I felt nervous all the time, and how I've been so hyper for the last few years. I told her how I felt so terrified whenever I got on the interstate, and that I had to get off at the first side road because things would be spinning so fast and I would get so anxious I felt like I might pass out at times. I told her about how my lower back hurt so badly, but the doctor couldn't find anything. I told her how I needed to take half an Ativan at night just so I could sleep.

She listened to my story patiently and sympathetically, and when I was finished, she asked me if I was thirsty. I was; I hadn't talked that much all at once in a long time. She got me a Coke from her refrigerator and I opened it. To this day, I think that was the best tasting Coke I have ever had in my life.

When I finished, Zelda asked me if I would like for her to read my palm. When I asked, she said she charged twenty-five dollars, so I agreed.

She took my hand and looked real close at all the lines. "You are going to meet a man and get married soon, but I don't think you should. You are very kind and well liked, but this man will treat you bad, and no one in your family will care for him." Then she went on to tell me, "You have been fooled many times by someone you trust in your family, but you can't see that because you love her. Do you have a sister?"

"Yes. Just one."

She went on with what she was seeing in my hand. "You have been hurt badly by your parents' divorce, and now it's hard for you to trust others or allow others to love you." Then she said, "Someone has worked something on you, and it will take a long time to get it off, and a lot of money. I can do the work if you want me to."

By then my head was spinning like a whirlwind, and I was ready to run out of there and never come back.

As I was leaving, she said, "Come back if you would like to talk more about how you are feeling."

I never went back. In fact, for some reason, I barely remembered the things she told me, though I did remember her warnings when it was too late.

I decided to stop at a store for a soda and pulled into the gas station to run in quick. Suddenly another customer came running in, yelling, "Lady, you got out of your car and just left it running. Look, your car has rolled out into the road and it's still going."

I ran as fast as I could to catch my car; it was my favorite, my sweet little blue Toyota. Thank God there was a curb and my car stopped rather than jump on over it. I jumped in and just kept driving, my reason for stopping in the first place utterly forgotten.

I remember one time my sister and I were visiting dad and it was icy. I always hurried, moving quick, and I stepped onto an icy patch and did the splits, falling right down, but it was like a bouncing ball, I was back up and hurrying to do whatever. My sister just laughed. Okay, most anyone might have laughed if they'd seen me, but I didn't think it was funny. Things were always happening crazy.

One day I was standing on dad's porch just talking and all of a sudden I lost my balance and just started to topple forward. Before anyone could react, I just rolled up in a ball and hit the ground. My dad was all concerned, asking if I was okay, but I just bounced up again like a Jack in the Box. I mean, how strange is that?

I went on working at the little barbershop run by the sisters. I made good money there; I really liked the place and the people. I continued living with my dad though he wasn't there much; he had a special lady friend he spent time with at her home after work. But we would talk over the phone, and in passing we would see each other and sometimes have dinner at home together if we had the time.

I was tired after standing all day and cutting hair, and my back would ache so bad. When I got home, I would usually head straight for the shower, grab a bite, and go to bed.

Chapter 5

One December night a girlfriend wanted me to do a perm for her at her house. We agreed that she would pay me later, but I wasn't really worried about it. Then about six months later, in May, she called me up and asked me to come by so she could pay me the money she owed me.

I stopped by on a Sunday evening, but after getting there I discovered she only had a hundred-dollar bill and neither of us had enough change. We walked over to a neighbor's house to see if he had enough.

About a week later my girlfriend called me up and invited me over to play some cards. She was going to have a few friends over. When I got there, that same neighbor who had the change was there too.

I didn't pay much attention to him, but I did notice that he kept staring at me, and when I started to leave, he asked me for my phone number. I was in a hurry; I was always in a hurry, so I gave it to him.

He did call me, and he asked me out, but me being so tired and always in some zone-land, I found myself spending a lot more time with him than I knew why; he was nothing special. I liked him, he was not especially handsome, but not bad looking, not especially charming, but he had an okay smile; I certainly didn't love him, but somehow, only four months later, I was telling my father that we were getting married.

I remember my dad just looking at the floor when I told him, like he would have liked to say something but wouldn't let himself. Dad had a lot on his mind. My brother was in jail for drugs and dad worried about him a lot.

This guy came over one evening. I was there, but I could only wonder why he'd come so out of the blue like that, but then I knew. He started chatting up my dad, getting all buddy-buddy with him, but I think my dad saw right through him. I think dad didn't like him being so much older than me. You know, I never did know how old he was, or even when his birthday was.

When the time came, dad just gave me enough money for a small church wedding at the Brookstown Methodist Church over in Pfafftown.

I called my sister and asked her what dress size she wore, and my best girlfriend as well, and I bought them pretty blue matching dresses. My wedding dress was off-white. Through the whole thing, I felt like I was a buzzing bumblebee in a fog, zipping around super-fast, not taking a moment to think about anything. I mean, I didn't really know this man very well. He was much older than I was, with some gray in his hair. He kept telling me I was getting old and needed to get married, but I was only thirty.

The wedding was planned for September 23, 1989, right after Hurricane Hugo, a category five storm, struck the east coast. If that wasn't an omen, I don't know what was. If I wouldn't listen to Zelda, I should have paid attention to this, but I couldn't pay attention to anything.

My oldest brother came to walk me down the aisle, but before we took our first step along that path, he asked me, "Do you want to change your mind?"

I thought, *Change my mind. I think I have lost my mind. Why am I getting married to this man? I don't feel like I know him well enough.* I felt like I was in a dream or maybe a nightmare. But all in a hyper fog, I found myself saying 'I do.'

We had a small party after the ceremony, with a wedding cake and lots of other food, and then I called my mom in Tampa Florida to tell her I was coming to bring my husband to meet her for our honeymoon. We were planning to go to Sea World and I wanted us to spend some time with her.

My new husband drove my nice little blue Toyota way too fast for me. I got so scared, I had to take half an Ativan and sleep for most of the trip. I hated that feeling. I hated drugs. I was either very hyper or zoned out like a zombie. One look from my mom said it all; we looked like father and daughter, but she never said anything out loud.

The day after the wedding, I woke up feeling like I'd been hit by a semi-truck. I took one look at this man and I couldn't imagine being married to him for the rest of my life. *What had I done?*

As I think back, why didn't my sister have a long talk with me? But she had no time for useless me.

Mom was nice, but she always seemed on edge. She wasn't at all happy about who I'd decided to marry, but I was married so she tried to make the best of it. She asked me once what my dad had to say about it, but he hadn't said anything either and I told her as much. My marriage wasn't but a couple days old and I was already feeling like I'd made a huge mistake.

Now that I was married, my husband was rapidly turning into a jerk. We went to Sea World and I wanted to buy me a Sea World T-shirt. I had over eight hundred dollars in my purse at the wedding, but when I opened it up to buy my shirt, I had not one dollar to my name. I asked him, "Where's my money?"

He said, "I will be handling all the money from now on. The man in the family does that."

I thought, *I have been single all my life and I took care of myself just fine. This is not going to work.*

We stayed in Florida for a week and I was seriously ready to go home by then. In fact, I was wanting to go back in time and undo it all, but that wasn't possible, so I tried to make the best of it.

We stopped by my sister's to pick up his dog—that's *his* dog, not *our* dog—and I overheard him saying to my sister, "I married the wrong sister." I thought, *You sure did.*

Home was a camper trailer like you can pull behind your car or truck, and it was parked down a dirt road over in Stanleyville. I took one look at this thing and thought, *This is not going to work for me.*

I went back to work at Third Generation, but then this guy I'd married—I won't even grace him with the name 'husband' anymore—came to my work, and in the middle of a cut, he told me I wasn't going to work there anymore, that this would be my last cut.

I'm sure everyone there, and for sure *I* thought, *How rude*, but he waited until I was done and then he made me pack my tools and leave. Boy was I upset. God help me, *please*!

I remember him telling my sister one day that since he'd married me, if anything happened to my dad, he would take over running the family.

I told him right then, "You will never make it that far in my life."

One day he tried to hold me down. He pinned me down so hard I thought he might have broken some ribs. I was so upset and now terrified; I fought for all I was worth and when I got away, I ran. I checked myself into the hospital. My ribs weren't broken, but my doctor knew me well, and he said, "Allison, you need to get away from him." He kept me in the hospital for about a week because I was so bruised up. Really bad bruises can be dangerous; I didn't know that until then.

Every day, that man would bring by hotdogs for lunch. He would buy them from Wilco Gas Station where he could get them two for a dollar. Then he went to Goodwill and bought me clothes. He gloated like he was being so generous, but I found the receipt.

Of all the people to come see me when I was in the hospital, my sister was not one of them. For the whole week that I was there, she did not stop by once. She said it was because she didn't want to run into him, but as God is my witness, if it was her lying in a hospital, I'd have been by her side as much as humanly possible. She was my sister, and sisters were supposed to do things like that for each other.

Despite all his other troubles, dad tried again to help me get on my feet, and on the promise that we'd pay him back, he loaned us enough money to make a down payment on a small home in the city. I should have never let it happen. I should have taken my doctor's advice, but I was so mixed up and so messed up.

This might have been a built-on-the-ground building, but it was no more a home than his little trailer on wheels. He was always telling me what to do and how to do it. I was scared most of the time. In an effort to make it something like a home, we adopted a dog from the Forsyth County Dog Shelter. He was such an ugly little mutt, but I loved him anyway. I named him Shaker.

I tried to visit my brother in jail as often as I could. It was always a struggle, doing anything I wanted to do. It didn't matter the reason.

One day this man who was supposed to be my husband came home and he knew who I talked to on the phone. I thought, *How could he possibly know who I'd talked to? He wasn't home.* I wasn't one to hide my phone conversations, but this was going too far, so I started looking. I found a cord hidden under the carpet leading to the basement. I followed it and it led to a tape recorder. He was recording any phone calls coming in or going out. I was so mad, but I just left it and found a hammer and laid it handy.

He came home, and after dinner, I said, "Can you come downstairs? I think the washing machine needs fixing."

He followed me down the stairs and I took up the hammer, and when he came around to the washer, I said, "Look here." And I smashed his recording device into a thousand pieces. I said, "You won't come home here anymore and give me a black eye because I talked to my family or friends. I'm through."

He looked so surprised, and guilty, but that's when I decided to leave.

I called my sister and asked her to come get me. I would have gone back to my dad's, but my brother was out of jail now and there wasn't room. My sister said, "Allison, I'll come get you, and I'll put you up, but you promise you won't go back." I got away with only the clothes I was wearing. I did go back though, to get things important to me, but I had to leave the dog; I couldn't take care of him.

I did manage to get my car, but he'd talked me into signing the title over to him, so one rainy night, when we were all sleeping, he came and took it back with a tow truck.

Feeling like I was high and frantically hyper all the time, worried about everything and nothing, I tried to do my best to earn my keep at my sister's house, I mowed her yard and cleaned her house until I could find a new job.

She wasn't easy to live with. She was very controlling. I could only take a shower once a day and laundry was done only on Saturday. She didn't want me to turn the heat up. Heat was electric and it cost a lot so we had a kerosene heater in the den. We had a five-gallon gas can and we would go to the store and buy kerosene for the heater. I remember the nights were so cold; it reminded me of that old house on Speas road when we were kids. The only difference was she had a heated waterbed so she was warm at night. I just had a regular bed and no heating blanket. Cold nights sure didn't help me sleep, and it didn't help my back any either.

I surprised her once. I found us both real pretty long gray overcoats for ten dollars each at a thrift store. It was a cold winter and we both needed coats. They were real nice coats and she actually like hers and smiled. I think that was the first time I'd ever seen her smile about something I did.

In the meantime, the turd I was married to kept calling, trying to talk me into coming back, but I wouldn't go. I'd had quite enough of him. He'd drive by every day too, trying to keep track of my every move. My sister didn't want me to go out at night and I didn't feel like it anyway. It was starting to feel like I was in another prison. We didn't talk about it much. Every time the subject even came close to coming up, her expression would be like, 'How could you have been so stupid?' She never quite said it though.

My sister asked dad once, "Do you think Allison and I will ever find the right men?"

Dad's reply was, "You don't know how to act, and Allison is too kind."

She just got a strange look on her face, but dad was right about me. I was way too kind; I needed to be tougher.

I finally had to hire an attorney and go to court to get my own car back—that was so hard, making those meetings without having a car. His attorney looked like he hated him for lying to him and making him lose the case.

When I got my car back, I discovered that the turd I was supposed to call my husband had bashed in the hood with a rock. It drove okay, but it was all messed up. I sold it to a neighbor for $800. My dad was so upset because he'd just fixed the clutch for me, but I wasn't thinking and the guy had the money, and my car wasn't pretty anymore, *he'd* messed it up. It was…soiled, in a way.

My sister worked at a Ford Dealership and she knew about all the new and used cars that go through there. She found me a big white Chrysler for $300. This was not the car for me, but I bought it anyway; I needed a car. I am a short lady and I could hardly see over the steering wheel, and it guzzled gas something fierce. But it was pretty white on the outside and pretty red on the inside. I guess my sister thought I needed a tank. She would always laugh when she got in because the passenger's seat was broken so whenever someone sat in it, they would go shooting to the back.

She found me another car more my size, a gray Hyundai. The only thing with this car is there was no air conditioning. Not unless you were driving at least fifty-five miles an hour with all the windows down. Well, you know me and driving fast. I needed air conditioning.

She found another car and my dad traded my little Hyundai in for a nice four-door yellow Nissan with a sunroof. This car could even talk. A nice lady's voice told you when the door was opened or if you left the key in the ignition. It also had a keypad on the door in case you had locked your keys in the car. I didn't have the money for the upgrade in wheels so I was to pay my dad payments.

I would go over to my dad's every Saturday with a payment, and then I would end up cleaning his house and washing his car.

He would say, "Allison, can't you just sit still?"

I'd say, "No. It's very hard for me to sit or stay and just talk." I talked so fast all the time anyway. I needed to be doing something all the time.

I remember one time when I was at my dad's, I wanted to show off the keypad. I tossed the keys into the car and locked the door. Wouldn't you know it, this time when I punched my code into the door, it didn't open. Dad got so upset. I was embarrassed, but I asked him to take me to a gas station so I could get a bar and break into my own car.

I loved that car. I was always washing it. Dad would say, "You're going to wash the paint right off."

One day when I was visiting my dad, my so-called husband called saying if I didn't come get the dog, he was going to kill it. Before I could make any kind of arrangement to get him, I found him dead on the side of the road by dad's driveway. I was so upset. I called the Forsyth

County Sheriff's Department they told me that since I couldn't prove he'd killed my dog, there was nothing they could do. They told me to just bury the dog.

Dad and I buried my Shaker in dad's back yard. I felt so bad, and still do at times. How could someone be so coldhearted? Shaker hadn't done anything wrong. I just couldn't stay there any longer. I never thought he'd kill the dog to hurt me. What kind of person thinks like that?

My sister's one hobby or interest seemed to be her Tarot cards and other things of that sort, so one day she took me to a meeting where all sorts of such people get together. I met this one lady who interested me right off. She did clairvoyant readings, and I got a card from her. A few days later, I gave her a call and asked how much she charged.

She told me she charged $75 an hour. With me not working that sounded like a lot, but I had it so I set up an appointment. She lived in Winston Salem, in a very nice area; the best part is that it wasn't far. I didn't have to use the interstate; that was a big plus for me. When I found the place, I saw this big red house, two stories tall. Just looking at the place made me feel warm and comfortable. I knew I was doing the right thing.

She and her big dog, introduced as Gabby, met me at the door. She was a soft-spoken woman, tall with a pretty smile. Hung all around her home were paintings she'd painted and they were all in bright warm colors.

Gabby followed us to the living room; he was so happy to meet someone new, but his was so big, he made me a little nervous; he also reminded me of my little shaker, having much the same coloring.

The lady sat me down and we started talking. She told me she was an art teacher at the local college, and that her husband worked for the airlines. She shared with me that she'd lost her sister and that her father wasn't doing well. I felt so sorry for her.

Then she asked if I knew anything about clairvoyant readings, if I'd had one done before.

I explained that I knew nothing about clairvoyant readings, but that I'd had many tarot readings from my sister. She was curious about that and asked how it went.

"She knows so much about me and I live with her. Are they real? Nothing ever seems to be in the right positions and they're always negative, and very upsetting." I went on to tell her that I didn't understand my sister in many ways, but I still loved her. She was just so different and it was hard living in her house.

She said, "I know your sister, not well, but I do know some of the ladies she took her Tarot card lessons with." She looked at me and then admitted, "I never would have thought you two were sisters."

I thought, *Here we go again.* My sister's standard response echoed in my ears as if she was standing right at my shoulder. 'I got the brains and she got the looks.' I told her what my sister always said, and she asked why she said that. "I suppose it's easier than admitting we had different dads."

She asked if I was comfortable and would I like something to drink, but I said, "No, I was fine."

Then she got down to business. She started to explain how a clairvoyant reading worked. I had long since developed the habit of sitting on my hands to keep them from shaking, but Gabby picked that moment to bark and I jumped. She just smiled and called him to lie down beside her. "There's a reason he's named Gabby," she said. "Don't be nervous about him; he really does like you." I could tell, but he was just so big and loud, and me being nervous all the time anyway, I couldn't help it.

Back to business. This lady said, "Clairvoyant means 'clear seeing in a neutral position.' It means using the power of the truth to see what is going on in the energy field surrounding the body called the aura."

I was so happy that she wanted to make sure I understood everything. She went on to explain that the reader has access to information in the aura as well as the major energies of the body. She stopped then and asked if I had any questions.

I shook my head and she continued. "Answers are found in the seven layers of the aura, with the truthful information that taps into the experiences that carry the energy of old memories from one experience to another, and from time to time." She told me that the information will identify my personality, and how that personality is activated in my relationship with others. "While I'm doing the reading, you may raise your hand and ask questions, or simply allow questions to evolve from your aura. You may find yourself with questions you didn't know you had. The most commonly revealed answers are such things as disharmony in relationships, career paths, life paths, and personal growth. Some of these paths continue from past lives, and from past experiences in this life. Some are dictated by your self-actualizing and self-limiting beliefs. All of this emerges to give you a reading that makes sense to you in terms of your present situation."

All I could think was, *Boy, that sounded like a lot to take in.*

After all that was carefully explained, she asked, "Are you still interested?"

My mind was flying like a jet trying to land in a hurricane. "I'm here. I'm trying to find out why I'm acting the way I do, so hyper and moving fast, and scared all the time. Do you think you can give me some advice?"

She smiled so kindly. "Yes, I can teach you how to slow down. And how to use the energies in different ways."

"Please help me. I really need help."

She curled up in her chair crossing her arms and tucking her legs up under her. I asked her how she could sit like that. She said she always sat that way; it was comfortable.

She closed her eyes and took a few deep breaths and then she started talking. She told me in my past life, I was a male barber living in another country far away, maybe Italy, and I knew everyone in the town. Men would share things with me in my little shop that I wasn't to share with others. She told me that I always kept their secrets. She told me I cut anyone's hair, rich man or poor man, even some who couldn't afford it. She told me I was very well known and liked.

She went on to describe what I looked like. I was average height, very neat, that I had dark black hair and a sharp-looking mustache. The ladies loved me. She told me I came from an average family of six, and that my folks had always made us work and earn our money. She said I was married and had a nice wife and three children. She went on to say I had tried to pick back up doing hair, but that I had some hard times and my energies had gone haywire. She explained that my mind jumped from thing to thing, person to person, and place to place. The energy levels would be so strong one moment and then get very low. She said, "I see you hurt in several different places in your body, mostly in your lower back, and yet I don't see you having ever been injured." She told me she could see something in my back, but she couldn't tell what it was.

She went on to tell me about the man I'd married in this life. She said he was a user and wanted money from my family, but that he wouldn't bother me anymore. He had moved on. She asked if he had remarried, and I said I paid for the divorce and he got married the next weekend. The lady had called me and told me so. I said it was a prayer answered, but he was now preying on someone else.

She went on to say that I was very kind and a giving person who loved people, loved to talk to people, that no person was a stranger. She said, "You believe in living and doing right by the laws of life." She described how my dad and I had always been very close and that he was still watching over me.

I asked her if I would ever get married again. She said, "That will be your choice. You have many to pick from, but you will learn many hard lessons beforehand.

She went on to say, "While you are living with your sister, it's like you jump from rock to rock in a flowing river. The rocks are slippery and every time you try to get things together, you slip and fall and she just watches. But I do see you getting stronger. You will move out and into a place of your own and you will get a job."

She told me that no one in my family understood me, my problem with being hyper and panicky. She said they wanted to help, but didn't know how.

I asked her about my sister. She said, "The best advice I can give you is to send her light and love. Every time you picture your sister in your mind, picture a big bright light shining down on her." She told me my sister is filled with jealousy because she sees herself as different from the family—that she refuses to see that the family loves her.

I said, "She is the only sister I have to look up to. She is my big sister, and I do love her. I just don't understand the things she says or the way she acts."

She stopped me and said, "One day you will."

I said in surprise, "I will?"

She just smiled and said, "You will understand many things you don't at this time. I suggest you start saying the Lord's Prayer out loud and very often. Think about what you are saying as you speak the words. This will help you."

She went on to tell me when it came to a man in my life, when I was ready, it would be like being in a horse stable with many doors to pick from, but this is a long way off. "You have many things to do to keep you busy before then."

She told me, "You have bright colors in your aura. You are very giving. If a rich lady wanted to give you $1000, it would be very hard for you to take it. In fact, you would get into an argument with the lady over her desire to just be nice and give you some money. You need to learn how to take as well as give." She went on to tell me that there was a man in my life, a good friend, who would be a friend for life. She told me he was my good friend in a past life too, but he was married. She asked me if I knew who she was talking about, and I did. He had always been a very good friend.

She paused for a moment and then she asked if I had any questions. I didn't so she said, "I will be closing now." She slowly opened her eyes and unfolded from the chair. She stood up and stretched and she even yelled real big. Then she smiled at me, a big friendly smile and said, "I want to say one last thing, Allison. It's okay to be happy and smile. You have a very pretty smile, and one day you will remember me telling you it's okay to smile in life and be happy."

I thanked her and she gave me a big hug and said, "If you need me, just call ahead."

I paid her and left. My head spinning all the way home. At some point I realized that I'd been there for three hours, but I'd only paid her the $75 she'd asked for.

My sister knew about my visit to the clairvoyant reader, and she wanted to know all about it.

I told her about how very different it was from her reading Tarot cards, and that I'd learned a lot, even about my past life. I told her she should go.

She didn't say a word, and never mentioned it again. It was okay for my sister to tell everyone's past and future, but she would never let anyone have a glimpse at hers.

I found a job at a girlfriend's store. She sold lady's clothes. She couldn't pay me much, but I worked hard. I helped ladies buy clothes and find things. I also helped with pricing and getting them all ready to hang out on the racks so they didn't look like they just came out of the shipping box. The job let me buy some nice pants and sweaters, and a few dresses.

As soon as I saved up enough money to pay the fees, my sister took me and a guy friend of mine all the way to Charlotte – an hour and a half drive – to retake my test for my barbering license. To maintain my license, I had to pay a yearly fee and my ex had forbidden it. It had been a good paying skill, so I tried for it again. The guy had volunteered to be my model, bless his heart. The interstate drive had me all wound up hyper and scared to death by the time we found the place.

There are seventeen steps to giving a man a straight shave and a short cut, and I couldn't make any mistakes. Even though my hands shook really badly, I made it through the test. License in hand, I went to work for the Parkway Barber Shop in Winston Salem. It was a nice shop; I was the only woman barber working there. I had plenty of clients and I was getting more each week. The pay for the cuts were cheap, but the tips were very good, me being young and pretty helped, I'm sure.

There was, however, a big problem with this place. The business was up for sale and two of the guys argued all the time over who was going to buy the shop. They both wanted it. One day, one of the guys told the rest of us that he was going to get his gun and take care of the other guy if he pissed him off again. I got so scared, and I'm sure the other barbers did too, but what with my back and my problem being hyper, I couldn't take the drama. It was as if I was scared all the time anyway, the last thing I needed was to actually *get* scared about something. It made my hyper brain go into overdrive, and I would nearly have panic attacks. I couldn't work in that kind of environment; I packed up all my tools and went to look for a job that offered insurance. I needed to find a better doctor. I needed to find out what was wrong with me.

I found a temporary job and McDonalds working from six in the morning until two in the afternoon, Monday through Friday. I made $6.35 an hour running the back grill for breakfast and through lunch. It didn't take me long to get tired of flipping burgers for next to nothing so I started looking again.

A little later I found a job way down in Kernersville, working in the office of Roadway Express Inc. It was only a temporary job, but they were paying me $10.00 an hour. I did lots of paperwork, filled out reports and made sure the computers didn't go down; if they did I had to call the support department and stay on the phone until they got back up and running. It wasn't a bad job, but the hours were terrible. I worked seven days on, seven days off, but the shifts rotated and sometimes I had to work nights. What with everything going on with my back and my trouble sleeping, changing my sleeping pattern was nearly impossible.

Now that I was making some good money, I paid my sister $75.00 a week to help pay some of the bills.

My sister said, "You need to keep this."

I said, "Take it. I can't continue to live here for free knowing bills come due every month."

One day, my sister decided she needed to do some outside repairs to her house. She didn't tell me a thing about it. I was just someone taking up the air she breathed;

she didn't need to tell me anything. So I come home from a long night's shift and went to bed exhausted, and then I was woken up by all this hammering going on outside. There was no sleeping through all that banging. It went on all day long.

When my shift came around again, I was nearly dizzy I was so tired. I couldn't drive like that so I called in. They fired me for not showing up. My sister didn't show the slightest bit of concern or regret that her repairs had cost me my job.

Even with my job, I worked hard. I tried hard to earn my keep in her house. I felt like I was just a slave to her, not a sister, not a person. In her eyes, I deserved no better consideration than she showed her washing machine.

There was always something going on with my sister at work. She'd be upset about something or someone and come home all in a fuss. I'd listen to it all. Sometimes I just wanted to say, 'Life isn't all about you,' but I never said it. I knew better. She was good at being negative. Finding the bad in anything.

Then there was a deal with her daughter and son-in-law; they were battling over something in court. I went with my sister to lend my support, but the trial ended up in a hung jury. That was a hard week. Every day when we got home my sister would go straight to her room and close the door. I tried to get her to talk about it, but I just got the silent treatment.

One day, out of the blue, she said to me, "Get out! Move!"

Chapter 6

It took a long time to get my head together and to accumulate enough money to get a place of my own again. My divorce was finalized in March of 1992 and I changed my name back to my maiden name.

I moved out of my sister's place in May of that year, into a small apartment in Winston Salem at Bethania Station Apartments for $375 a month. She didn't even offer to help with the move. It was like she wanted to be shut of me as soon as possible. It felt so good to be out on my own. I was so ready to get out from under my sister's controlling thumb; I just couldn't deal with her drama. Just getting back to being independent again felt like such a big move forward in my life, but I was still a mess. I was still in a hyper fog. Strange thing is, she knew how messed up I was, but she never stopped by or called to see if I was doing okay. She didn't have any time for me, and yet I always made time for her. I'd take her shopping whenever she wanted to go. She said to me once, "I don't mind going, but I don't want to go like we're on fire."

That apartment was probably the worst apartment in the city. The neighbor had cats and they never changed the litter box. The smell was so strong it seeped through the wall and made me sick. I even got a lung infection that nearly put me in the hospital.

I found another apartment back in Rural Hall at Providence Manor Apartments, for $305 a month, but it was way back in the back of the complex, and there were no outside lights. If I thought cats were bad, the guy who lived under me scared the begeebees out of me. I think he was a Vietnam Vet, but he was really messed up. He would always stare at me—just stare. It was freaky the way he looked at me.

He did the strangest things. He'd always take his sofa and chairs outside and beat them with a broom, not a bad idea if you can do it, but then he'd leave them out there until the manager of the complex made him put them back inside.

My sister brought me a black puppy, but I was scared to take him outside at night to go pee so I gave it to my sister's oldest son; his kids loved it.

I hated living there. I'd come home from work and run upstairs, hurry to get in my door and quick lock it again once I was inside. I even went to a pawnshop and bought me a little 38 special and I carried it in my purse. I was a nervous wreck. Well, I was already a nervous wreck, but being scared made it ten times worse.

One night I heard something outside, and I saw this man out on the railroad tracks with a BB gun and a big flashlight. I couldn't tell if he was going to kill the train or try to rob it. Thank God the conductor saw him in time and was able to stop. There were police cars and flashing lights all over the place after that.

I put in for a two-bedroom up front, but had to wait until my lease was up. That was a long year.

When my lease was finally up, for $375 a month I got my two-bedroom clear on the other end of the complex and the best part is that there was this bright shining light outside. For that alone the increase in rent was worth every penny. My accident-waiting-to-happen ex-neighbor can stay in his dark corner.

I was barely scraping by, but I was making it. Mom and I frequently called or wrote letters. But in 1994 mom got sick. It was cancer and she decided she had to move to a rest home. That January, my sister, my middle brother, and I went down to Tampa and packed up all her things and helped her move. She was so skinny and sick. Her last words to me were, "My little Allison, tell your dad I always loved him."

I wanted to stay, but I didn't have any money for a place and we had to get back. I was so poor I had to ask the church for money to pay my electric bill and buy some food. All the while mom's message to dad weighed on me. I didn't know how to tell him. I didn't want to give him her message over the phone; that wouldn't be right, but getting away to see him was hard. Eventually I called and told him. The line went so still. "Dad? Are you there?"

Mom passed away March sixth 1995. It was like us losing her all over again, but at least this time it was closure and not just her vanishing. We brought her back home for memorial services—they were held on a Sunday—on my birthday. Now, every year on my birthday, I remember how God took all my mom's hurting and sickness away and took her to heaven. I think of her often.

After mom passed, I started picking up my sister for church. It was the same church she had attended many years ago over in Pfafftown. It was a very small church, but a pretty place and the folks were very nice; they really loved God. It was a twenty-minute drive, but I didn't mind picking up my sister. We took turns driving.

For the next two years, I struggled so hard. I kept losing jobs, my back hurt all the time, sleep was a far-away wish, I worried about every little thing my chaotic mind lit on for more than a moment. Most of all I worried about how I was going to make ends meet.

Whenever I talked, I sounded like a record turned on high speed. The words would come tumbling out in a jumble, not always in any kind of coherent order; it was actually hard for me to recount an event in order. Dad would say, "Allison, slow down." What I said wasn't always nice either. I never thought about what fell out of my mouth, how it might hurt feelings. If I felt the need to say it, it would come, even if I interrupted whoever I was talking to. I couldn't help it. I couldn't stop myself.

I was all rush-rush on foot, but get me in a moving car and I became terrified. My stomach would churn to the point of throwing up if the car was moving much faster than I could run, and I wanted to crawl under the seats and hide if we were driving in the city, the buildings all looked so huge and tall, and it felt like they were all going to fall over on me.

My sister would say, "Allison, you never just sit down and rest. You're always going like a mad woman." That wasn't quite true; I could sit still, but I knew it wasn't the normal kind of sitting still. At times I could sit and look at something forever without blinking, like I was a robot suddenly just turned off, but if I was moving at all, it was at super high speed, like I was running, only I wasn't. From the moment I opened my eyes in the morning, it was zoom-zoom. I'd race around and clean the house, mow the yard, weed the garden, wash my car, wash the dog, just go-go-go; even if none of it needed to be done, just to keep moving. Every little thing had to be just so too—perfectly so.

If I was standing in line somewhere, like at the grocery store, I always felt like everyone was staring at me up and down, seeing all my faults and mistakes, judging me. It was a living hell. I'd ask the person in front of me if I could go before them. I hated just waiting; I had no patience. I had to be moving all the time.

During interviews, I would sit on my hands so they wouldn't notice how bad my hands were shaking. I sounded nervous enough; I didn't need to look like I was terrified.

Whenever I tried to talk to my sister about my problem, all she would say was, "This shall pass too." What does that mean? That was no help. Besides, it never passed. Did she think this problem I had was just going to go away because she declared it? I could only wish it was so, but all I could see was that it was getting worse all the time.

A lady at the church my sister and I was going to found me a job at a rental store. She obviously did not know this man. The owner was rude to the ladies and he was always drunk. He'd be drinking up in his office all the time. He called me up there one day and started talking all kinds of nasty stuff about sex and on and on.

I left and quit as soon as I could clear the door. I went straight away and got me an attorney. We went three different times to speak to a counselor. She told me she was pretty angry about the way this man was treating employees and that I did the right thing. I even told his wife what happened and she was going for a divorce, so my case helped her too.

While I was seeing this councilor, she asked if she could give me a test; she said it would show how I think. When she got the results, she was very surprised, and very pleased as well. It seems not many women had a brain that worked the same as mine did. She said I could think like a woman and like a man. She said it was a special gift. I was sure shocked to hear that, but I was happy and thankful too.

I showed the results to my sister, but she didn't say anything. I mean she didn't say anything at all. She could have said 'that's nice, Allison.' Heck, she could have said, 'I don't believe a word of it.' but no, she said nothing at all. It would have been acknowledging that her favorite saying of 'she got the brains but I got the looks' wasn't entirely true. She couldn't have that.

I went on with my attorney to sue my ex-boss for sexual harassment and we won $17,000, or one year's wages. Of course the attorney got half of that, but I was still able to pay a few bills.

I found a job at Amp Inc. It was a factory making electronic parts for computers. They paid $9.75 an hour. It was a temporary job. To get hired full time you had to prove yourself and come to work every day and put in full ten-hour shifts. I did that faithfully for a whole month, but I never got hired full time. I was fast too; the guy who worked beside me would say, "You work so fast, you could do my work and yours too." Sometimes I did, while he was on break. I liked him; he was a good coworker, nice looking, but way too young for me.

I told my boss one time, "Heck, if you can't hire me full time, maybe I need to look for a smart, good-looking engineer in here." Nice pipe dream, but I knew better. Work was work and play was for after work and I didn't play. I just worried, and I was always tired. I shook like I was on a drumhead someone was strumming, just constantly vibrating. After thirteen months the job ran out. I thought, *What next?*

I drew my unemployment and started job-hunting again. A good friend told me about a clerical job at an insurance office as an assistant, so I applied and got the job. Come to find out the lady I was working with was changing all the numbers to make her and the main boss' sales numbers look good to the home office. I worked there for about six months.

I also got a part time job in the evenings at the UPS Hub. The job was keying in corrected addresses and putting labels back on the package to be placed on the belt to be sent out the next day. I will tell you though, the noise and the trucks flying by was hard on me, but they paid $10.00 an hour so I tried very hard. Lifting heavy packages with my back killing me certainly didn't help.

Dad got sick during the summer of 1997. At first he was in denial and very depressed. The doctors called the whole family together in his room and told us all the bad news: dad only had three months to live. The cancer had started in his lungs and spread rapidly from there. We were all stunned and devastated. But while the doctor was talking, my sister was sitting facing away from dad, facing me, and she was making faces trying to make me laugh. This was no laughing matter. Dad got so angry with me he told me to go home, and he used a few cuss words to do it. I was so angry and upset, when my sister and I got out in the hall I told her, "That isn't funny. You make me sick, acting so stupid." Oh I was so furious at her.

I'd just lost both my jobs again, so I mostly closed up my apartment and moved in with my dad to take care of him. Getting unemployment let me keep my apartment, but I was staying with dad nearly all the time. Dad couldn't stand the smell of food or cologne or perfumes—anything that had an odor, so I would cook meals at home and take them over.

At first he didn't understand why I was doing all this for him, going to all this trouble. As he saw it, I had completely halted my life to take care of him. He thought the hospice was paying me to stay, but no. I explained, "You are my dad. You took care of me while I was growing up. It's only right that I take care of you now. I can and you need me."

The days were long, and the sickness just kept coming day after day with no better days in between. I did my best, I'd run to fix a meal, give him his meds on time, take him to his appointments, and keep track of what the doctors told me to share with the family. We were in and out of the hospital like it had a revolving door.

One day as we were leaving the hospital, I ran ahead to bring the car around and a security guard was pushing the wheelchair; he accidentally bumped the door. My dad having bone cancer, his leg just broke right there as I was walking up. It made a horrible sound, and then my dad was grabbing his leg and yelling in pain.

I grabbed the wheelchair, telling everyone to get out of my way and I headed as fast as I could for the emergency room hollering for help. The nurses picked him straight up out of the wheelchair. All I could say was, "Just hold my hands." I felt so bad for him. As if the cancer wasn't bad enough—now this. Cancer: I *hate* that word.

They rushed him into surgery and put a rod in his leg. When he finally got to a room, I was there and I wasn't going anywhere. All the family was calling in or visiting, feeling bad for him. For my sister to come see him, I had to go get her; she didn't like parking at the hospital.

They sent us home after a couple days. There was nothing more they could do for him—he was not getting better. We would sit on the porch—there was a ramp there now, for the wheelchair, built by the Reynolds Volunteers from the hospice; they were so nice. We would sit on the porch; I would enjoy the sun beating down on me and he would have an umbrella. Family, friends, coworkers, and neighbors would drop by and sit a while, and the pastor of the hospice and our church would come often. It all cheered him up so much. I would always fix lots to eat because some of them would stay for the meal. Dad would always say, "Who is going to eat all that food?"

I said, "Whoever shows up hungry."

I learned all the TV shows he liked to watch and when they were on; I also quickly learned those he didn't like; that was a big deal. It got to be somewhat funny when something he didn't like would come on; I'd immediately go over and change the channel. He never had to say, "Allison, change the channel." Or "Allison, isn't there anything else on?"

Dad was always thrifty. He liked his tea just so. Boy, don't put more than two ice cubes in his glass. He didn't like too much water melting into his tea.

I took care of him like a baby. His legs would get so swollen and his feet so tight-looking by the end of the day. I would rub them down with lotion and put soft white socks on his feet.

We had a nurse come in three times a week, and a certified nurse assistant to help give him a bath every day, a physical nurse to help with getting him up and around. With my back always hurting, I couldn't do the heavy lifting. I learned to work with the hospice giving him all his meds on time and getting him to all his doctors' appointments every day. Most importantly, I had to keep a ledger accounting of it all; the hospice made it clear they would check behind me, so things had to be written down. My back was killing me and my hyper, wound up brain was robbing me of anything that might resemble sleep. My hands and feet were swelled up every morning, feeling like nails were poking through the tops, and my periods were vicious. I would bleed so bad, and my back would cramp up with muscle spasms in just the one place. I would need to bend over sometimes just to stretch out the cramp in my back. Sometimes I had to go lay down on my stomach and wait for the pain to let up.

The doctor gave me water pills for my swollen feet, but that only made my skin feel dryer than it already was. I felt like I was swimming in skin lotion, my skin soaked it up like a dry sponge, but my skin took on a yellowish cast and was even gray in places. My eyes were sore and red all the time. I had to wear Chap Stick or lipstick all the time or my lips would peel and bleed. Even though my body felt like a dried up desert, if I was working in the yard on a warm day, sweat would pour off me like I was standing in the shower. It all made no sense to me. I was exhausted all the time, but I had to carry on.

Most of the family would come by, some to help with dad and to give me a break to go check my mail or just to do some real thinking or praying. My prayer was always, "God, please don't let my dad suffer any more than he has."

Provided there wasn't some work-related issue, my sister would come by on weekends, and occasionally she would spend the night, but the things she deemed important or not important sometimes astounded me. Dad was dying, but she couldn't take off from work to spend some time with him, or even evenings for that matter. So what if he wasn't *her* dad, he was the only dad she ever knew. But I never said anything; dad liked her gravy, and I never was very good with gravy.

My uncle, one of my dad's oldest brothers, would drive up every day like clockwork at nine o'clock in the morning, rain or shine. Dad took to calling him my buddy. "Here comes your buddy," he'd say. I could depend on him for anything I asked.

I would just smile and say, "Yep, he's coming to check on us."

One day my oldest brother came by one time to spell me and said, "Ms. Neat, I can't find anything." Well, when you put things away, that's where you find them.

It didn't matter all the hard work, all the pain, all the worry. It was a joy during this time in my life, to take care of my dad. I came home from one of my short breaks to see all three of my brothers sitting watching TV with dad. As soon as he saw me, dad sat up straight and asked, "Are you my girl?"

I would have crawled right up in his lap like I did when I was little if I dared. "I'll always be your girl, dad."

Things like that will never be forgotten; they are the kinds of things you hold onto for the rest of your life.

Nights were hard. I learned what to do, but if I needed help I would call the hospice nurse. They were an awesome group of folks.

There is a woman from Walkertown who was a friend of mine from way back when I'd owned my house out there. One Saturday, when my sister was taking me to run some errands, she took us over to her place; she was staying with her parents who were getting up there, caring for them. She had several cats and dogs, and sometimes I'd give her some money to feed them. Once I gave her money to buy some tires for her car, they were so worn. She read playing cards for a living and sometimes it paid well and sometimes it didn't. Sometimes she'd call me and ask me to bring her something from the store she'd forgotten to pick up.

She'd never seen the two of us together before, and how my sister came to know her, I never knew. She was surprised at how different we were. My sister said her favorite thing. "She got the looks and I got the brains."

My friend just laughed it off like she knew better. She told my sister that the man she loved would come back into her life.

We both knew who she was talking about, but he'd gone back to his first wife, and her and my sister got along like a match gets along with gunpowder, so we had our doubts. She wasn't reading cards; we were just talking on her porch. Before we left, my sister handed her a hundred-dollar bill. That really surprised me. Why would she give her so much money? Maybe she owed it to her for something else.

Getting to know this woman better was slow, but she was a light in my darkness that just kept getting brighter. I felt like she was actually listening to me when we talked. We'd talk on the phone, and she'd tell me things. One day she told me I would find out the truth about a lot of things that had been done behind my back, but she wouldn't tell me what. She knew things were bad with me, and she told me she would pray for me. She also told me that I had such a kind spirit, and she said once that my sister's was so different, but she wouldn't tell me what she meant by that.

She also told me about a guy friend of mine, how he would be a friend for life, and he is and always has been. I met him at a local airport while flying in one day with my pilot friend. I gave him a card to come get his hair cut and we've been friends ever since.

With my dad, May turned into June which turned into July, and the doctor had said only three months, but I am certain God had other plans. August came and went and so did September.

Dad passed on November seventh of 1997 at home. A hospice nurse and I were with him. I thought my heart would break.

After the funeral service, my sister surprised me by coming to stay a couple nights with me. She didn't have to, but it was nice of her. I was used to picking up the pieces of my life, and now I had to get out there and make my way again.

I took some time to rest and get my thoughts together, and then I started looking for another job. My oldest brother wrote me a very nice letter. He was very concerned for me. He sent me a tape to listen to by Dr. Norman Vincent Peale, a minister and author of The Power of Positive Thinking. The name on the tape was Why Some Positive Thinking Gets Powerful Results; it came out in 1987. It was a very helpful tape. I would pop it into my cassette player in my car and listen to it as I went looking for jobs, and I am sure it helped me get many of my jobs. I was also certain that God had his hand on me and that my dad was watching over me; I could feel him sometimes.

I went to work at my sister's place running a switchboard. The job was okay, but the other people who worked there took to complaining to me about my sister. I'm just her sister, what could I do? They would tell me how we were so different. It was like they expected me to intercede for them with my sister, but there was no way; I didn't even try.

I had some money from dad and now that I had a job, I sold my little yellow Nissan and bought a Ford.

One Sunday afternoon in June, my friend from Walkertown called me and invited me to a revival in Greensboro. I asked if she minded if I invited my sister to come along.

The revival was so inspiring. The prophet spoke the word of God with such passion and such conviction. It filled my heart to near bursting. He also called people up front, and after making sure we all knew there was no way they knew him, he would prophesize over them. I swear the man was touched by the Lord.

Later when the basket was passed around, my friend and I both put a little cash in, but my sister didn't part with a dime.

When we were leaving the tent, a man came at us from clear across the grounds. He walked straight up to my sister, touched her on her forehead, and said, "I rebuke you, devil, in the name of Jesus."

My sister fell down to her knees and started sobbing.

I was so shocked, and our friend was too. What in the world was this all about? What is going on?

My sister got to her feet and the man said he would pray for her and then just left.

When we got to the car, my friend told us that she'd seen him before; he was a minister of a well-known church in town.

I just looked at my sister. She was too upset to drive so she was sitting in the back seat. She looked like she might start crying again. I said, "Are you okay?"

She mumbled something like, "Yes, I'm fine."

I knew she was lying, but I didn't dare ask again. By then I was on the interstate of terror so I had to concentrate and try to keep my heart from pounding its way out of my chest.

One night my sister called me and told me the owner of the dealership where she worked had told her to tell me to find another job. Just like that, out of the blue. It was okay with me though; I really hated the way everyone wanted me to be the middleman with my sister. The next day I just picked up my things and drove away without saying anything to any of them. I got in my car and the perfect song was on the radio. *Take This Job and Shove It* by David Allan Coe. That song made my day; I rolled down my window and turned the volume up. I have lost many a job in the past and I would find another one.

A few days later, my sister stopped by as if everything was just the way they used to be, or were supposed to be, in her eyes. She told me that the general manager had been fired too, and after having worked there for seven years, but she didn't care; she didn't like him anyway. They replaced him with some guy that had worked there before; she really liked him. Apparently he'd mentioned his wife needing a nanny to take care of their two-year-old son. The job would pay $150 a week.

I figured I still had some money left in my savings, so the extra would allow me to take a little more time to find my next job. I went to the boy's birthday party to meet him. He's such a cute, sweet little boy, so I take the job as his full time nanny during the day. My hours were from 7:30 in the morning until mom got home at five in the evening. My job was to get him up in the morning, feed him breakfast and then take him to school and pick him up at 12:30 sharp. He was a real joy. I loved dressing him up, and he would look for me every morning.

I had to keep a tab on everything we did, what he ate and what we did in the afternoon. I would take him to their country club to swim, and we would eat at the snack bar there. We played some in the yard, and I would read to him while rocking him to sleep for his nap. His two grandmas would come by often to visit and play with him.

When it came to what this only child needed, no expense was spared. I really liked that. The only bad part was my back of course. If he fell asleep downstairs, I had to carry him up to his bed. Carrying him hurt my back like there was a knife in there digging around, so I tried my best not to have to carry him anywhere.

I also took lots of pictures, but I didn't mention those. When Christmas came around, I had all those pictures developed and I bought a Snoopy photo album. I also did small ones for the grandparents. When the mom opened her Christmas present and saw that photo album, I could tell from the look on her face, that was the best present under the tree. There on those pages were all the things she missed when she was off at her school.

However, $150 a week wasn't paying my bills and I was running out of money. I asked the lady if I could do more while I was there. I offered to do the ironing. She already had a lady come to clean, and there was another night nanny. I did some of their ironing, but still it wasn't enough.

The job ended one morning after eight months when the husband yelled at me because I asked him if he knew who had done the ironing the night before. It was an innocent enough question; he had no call to yell at me. So I kept my mouth shut, and I just turned off the stove, collected my purse and jacket, and walked out the door.

He was an honest man though. He'd taken good care of me while I worked there. I bought the gas I used to take their son where we went, but he paid for an oil change and put new tires on my little Ford. He also sent me two extra paychecks through my sister. I didn't expect that, but he said that was the agreement and wouldn't take them back.

I got a job at Clear Channel Inc. Radio Station working afternoon's part time as their switchboard operator. That job also let me go along on a remote show for like when a new store opened; we would hold a show at the store to draw in business. It was a lot of fun. I also would get into concerts for free if we were covering them at all.

It was a great job and I really liked it, but it was only part time and not enough to pay the bills, so in September of 1999, I found a full time job as a bank teller at BB&T Bank. All I can say about that job was that it was full time. I met lots of people and ran into some old friends and business owners I knew, which was nice.

That October, my apartment complex came under new management and I was given a week to get out, and right after I'd gone to all the trouble of painting too. I found a little efficiency over on Hanes Mall Road for $385 a month, and took a couple days off to move. I called a moving place and they brought a truck and trailer over. Four nice guys came in and loaded all my stuff up in no time. The apartment was much newer and warmer, and the complex had a nice pool and a tennis court.

I called the Winston Salem Journal asking the columnist, Dear Sam, could I be forced to move from a place where I'd lived from 1992 until 1998? I'd always paid my rent on time and I'd done some upgrades at my own expense too. Dear Sam wrote back in the morning paper saying I could have sued the realtor and that I wouldn't have had to stay there to do it, but I didn't try.

They did me a favor; the place was falling down around my ears anyway. They did give me back my deposit. $350 helped to pay a few bills.

My sister had come to help with the move, and when we got everything into the new place, we sat down for a break. She looked at me and said, "You are going to meet a man that you like while living here."

I asked, "How would you know that?"

She just said, "Don't ask me how I know."

I worked at the bank for a year before I turned in my notice. Anymore, sitting or standing, my back hurt all the time, and my hyper chaotic brain was wearing me down. I was *Running on Empty*, as the song goes. I couldn't even just look at something for more than a second or two; my eyes were always darting all over the place. I'd have panic attacks at the drop of a pin. The mere thought of driving on the interstate, or at all fast, brought one on.

I had to find some relief somewhere. Something was wrong with me and I had to figure out what it was before I died from it. I was that wore out. I'd go home and soak in the bathtub for hours; that was the only thing that seemed to slow me down some, but I couldn't live in a bathtub. It made no sense. I had to figure this out and do something about it. Now with both mom and dad gone, I felt very vulnerable, isolated, and afraid. It just wasn't right.

Chapter 7

After quitting the job at the bank, I started to do lots of real serious thinking and praying to God to show me what is making me like this. I hadn't been like this forever, but for a long time things hadn't felt right. I was always worried about everything and anything, but there was no real reason to be so worried. I lived alone, I didn't date, and I hadn't been out partying for a long time. Now that I wasn't working, I was even more alone.

I had some unemployment coming so I went and signed up for it. Since I had quit or resigned at the Bank, I had a waiting period to get a little money, but I had some in savings so that was covered for a little while. I had to find out what and how a person would move and feel the way I did for such a very long time. None of it made any sense. I felt like I was a puppet on strings, or even possessed by a demon. Now that was a thought.

One day, I was waiting for my sister to come pick me up to go shopping at Wal-Mart only she was about an hour late. My sister? Late? Now I had cause to worry. My sister may have no consideration for me, but she was usually on time.

When I finally do get a call from her, she starts out with, "Oh you won't believe who I have been talking to, my old boyfriend."

I knew immediately who she was talking about; the guy who had gone back to his ex-wife more than ten years ago. It seems that this wife had passed away from breast cancer eighteen months ago, and he just happened to be in the neighborhood checking on a job down the street. She told me she'd gone out to check the mail. All I could think of is, *why would she be checking the mail today? It was the 4th of July. There was no mail delivery on the 4th; it was a national holiday.*

Oh my, I thought, *and now he's back looking to hook up with Ms. I-hate-every-man-I-ever-ran-into-but-not-him.* Well we would see. Oh well, he'd never done anything bad to me and dad seemed to like him; he'd done some good work for dad a while back. "Time will tell, true love never ends," I said. "I wish you happiness in the days to come. I wish only the best for you both."

When she finally got over to pick me up, she filled me in on how nice he was, and how pleasant it was to see him and what all. She was so happy she was bouncing like a schoolgirl going out on her first date.

I just thought to myself, *If this news would have been mine to her, she would have found all the negative in the world to spew back at me, and a whole string of smart remarks to follow*, but I just listened and wished her the best.

Then I remembered what our friend back in Walkertown had said, and now it had come true. This got me to thinking. Sure meeting up with this old lover was something to feel happy about and I was happy for her, but the only reason he was available again was because his wife had died. Not only that, but she had died a long and horrible death from cancer. That was nothing to be happy about.

Now don't get me wrong, my sister and that woman absolutely hated each other with a passion, and I never knew why. She would throw underwear in my sister's front yard and call her up on the phone and leave a message saying, 'You are a witch. You got your black pot out in your back yard?' She even sent my sister a cross in the mail once; my sister burned it and then buried it in the back yard. One night, she hung a sheet up on a big board near my sister's house. She wrote bad names all over it. Anyone driving by could read it. Between those two women there was out-and-out war from Lewisville to Rural Hall. I never met her, but the war ended with her death and now my sister was all happy, not at all sad that someone he'd loved was now dead.

I asked my sister, "Did you know she was going to die?"

My sister looked right at me and said, "Oh no."

I thought, *Right, like all the other things you didn't know.* It all made me think of another of my sister's favorite sayings. "I can make your life miserable and never touch you." I heard her say that way too many times while living at her place.

Being alone, and under the influence of my old friend and my church, I started praying a lot. At first I'd try to kneel by my bed, but then I'd find myself popping up like a Jack in the Box and doing something else. I couldn't focus on my words and it was impossible to remain still. Then I had an idea. The only place in the world where I could remain quiet for any length of time was in the bathtub. My bathtub became my prayer closet, and among my prayers was a fervent thank you God for providing me with a big water heater. I was even thankful for the nice tub in my little efficiency apartment; I spent a lot of time there. It became my hiding place; if you needed me, you could always find me there. It got to where I would sit in the tub to look for jobs in the want ads or talk to friends on the phone. I knew this wasn't right though, so I would call my old friend from Walkertown.

She was a very devout woman and I know I drove her crazy by calling, but she was such a comfort to talk to. She said one time, "Allison, I would cuss you out for calling all the time if I didn't like you so much."

I couldn't get mad when she said that. I knew I was making her nervous, my calling so much, but I think she understood how important it was for me to just hear her voice. Talking to her felt like there was one person inside my glass bubble of craziness who understood the words coming out of my mouth. Sometimes *I* didn't even understand myself.

One Saturday afternoon, she called me. She told me the prophet was back in Greensboro and she wanted to know if I would pick her up and go with her.

Remembering the drive on the interstate I talked it over with her. She said she knew a back way. That meant no interstate; I was so relieved.

That Sunday, May 9, 1999, I got my nerves all together and picked her up and headed over to Greensboro. It was all I could do to keep from having a panic attack even though we weren't on the interstate, but I really wanted to go.

We had left early enough to stop and have lunch at Cracker Barrel and while we were there, I asked if she thought I might be called up this time.

My friend's reply was, "Let's pray. If it is God's will tonight, this prophet will call you out."

So we started praying, if it is God's will, amen.

There were a lot of people gathered there by the time we arrived, but even though we were thirty minutes late, we managed to get seats way in the back, right in front of the guy filming the whole thing.

The poor tent was really rocking with some good old southern gospel singing, and folks were standing and praising God. It all reminded me of going to church with my Aunt Sally. I joined right in, singing with all my might.

Where we were sitting, way in the back in straight chairs, it was hot with the sun beating down, but being way in the back like that, I could stand up and see better, and not be in someone's way. I was brought up to stand up for the Lord, or if good singing in the Lord's name was going on.

When the singing was over, the prophet said, "God has laid it on my mind and in my heart to call out seven people tonight."

My friend started praying. She got down on her knees beside her chair and was praying real hard.

With my heart in my throat, I watched him call people forward or go to them if they were in the front. He told them different things and laid hands on them, praying, telling them God worked through him. He even asked those he was speaking to, "Do I know you?" It was so very inspiring, so incredibly moving. I just knew that this man really worked for the Lord, and God was really working through him. He had a gift.

My eyes jumped all over the place, and I so wanted to be running or jumping, or moving somehow, but I watched and listened to every word that came out of his God-given mouth.

When it got down to him calling up the last of the seven he'd said he'd call tonight, he was looking around, and even way back to where we were standing, and then he pointed right at me. "The lady in the green dress, come up here, please."

My heart was beating like a drum on a football field at halftime. I almost couldn't breathe; he was talking to me. I gripped my hands together and put them right up under my chin like I was praying.

When I reached the front, he said, "I don't know you and I never met you, but I do know the voice of the Lord."

I just nodded; I could feel what he said was true.

All I could say was, "Praise God in the name of Jesus."

Then he said, "Are you ready?

I nodded and said, "Yes," but I'm not sure the word got out.

The prophet told me to lay my hands on my chest, then he placed his hand on my head and said, "You will never go under a knife, and you will never take chemotherapy. God is your chemotherapy and the hurt that someone put in your heart twenty-one and a half years ago will be gone, forever and ever. I pray that you are healed from the top of your head to the bottom of your feet. You are filled with the Holy Ghost, in Jesus' name, I pray. Amen."

Then the prophet looked at me and said, "Do you know how many years I said?

"I looked at him and said, "Twenty-one and a half years."

Then he said, "God has touched you from the top of your head to the bottom of your feet, in the name of Jesus."

Then he looked out in the crowd and pointed at my friend and said, "You have the blessing coming."

He looked across the crowd. "Is there anyone with this young lady?"

My friend raised her hand and said, "Yes, I am with her."

He asked her, "Have I ever talked to you?"

She said, "No, you haven't."

The prophet looked at me, his eyes were so intense and yet gentle. He told me to go give her a big hug because she had a blessing coming.

I did as I was told. I didn't know what to think. My heart was filled with so much joy at that moment.

I asked my friend what she thought her blessing might be, but she just said, "I have no idea. We must wait and see what happens, by the grace of God."

Then there was more singing. I was the last person to be called up—number seven. Being the seventh one was special to me. According to the King James Bible, the number seven has a meaning, which refers to the number of God, and divine perfection or completeness. On the seventh day, God rested after completing creation.

After it was all over, I told my friend, "I must have a copy of this." I asked her to wait, and I went to figure out how I could get a copy of this revival.

I walked around to the back of the big tent all alone, and then I felt like a surge of lightning went through my body. It was such a rush from the top of my head to the bottom of my feet. I just stopped and stood for a second, and then I went to find the trailer where the cameraman was.

I asked him if there was a way to get a copy of the film.

He told me he could do it, but that there'd be numbers running across the bottom.

I told him I'd pay him for a copy and he said he'd have it for me in about thirty minutes, so I waited. I paid him $50 for this golden piece of a miracle in my life.

I found my friend and we got back in the car. Forgetting about back roads, I headed for the interstate. I said, "This has been a great night."

She knew I was happy. God had answered our prayer. What a wonderful feeling, knowing God saw me here and helped me. Touching me to let me know he was with me.

I was tired, and as I was driving along, my friend was talking. I felt like a ton of bricks had been lifted from my shoulders. I had no idea what was going to happen in the future, but I know something profound had changed. God was watching over me, and God doesn't play.

I asked my friend what she thought about it all.

She said, "God is in control. You'll just have to wait and see." She also said, "God is awesome. When God does something, he does it right. You have a sweet spirit, Allison, and I like you a lot. You're a good person." I thanked her, but she added, "But you are so hyper and seem to need to slow down."

I told her I would do my best, and I meant it.

I dropped her off and went home. It was dark and the streetlights were lighting my way to my door, which was right by my parking place. I liked this new apartment. It had more than just a great bathtub and a big water heater.

Now, safe in my apartment, I started to think. The prophet had said that someone had put hurt in me twenty-one and a half years ago. That's twenty-one and a half years of my life gone forever. Who would want to do that? He'd said, someone had put hurt in me, but I had never really been hurt. My brain was so scattered still. All I could think of was to share with my sister.

My sister and I went to the same church, called Doub's Chapel, out in Pfafftown. So I got up early the next morning and picked up my sister. On the way, I started telling her all about my previous evening at the revival. I was still so excited about it, but she wasn't, not at all. She just sat there through it all without saying a word, not nodding, not smiling—nothing. I thought maybe she doesn't believe me, so I asked her to come over sometime, and I'd show her the tape.

She agreed and came over a few days later. I played the tape for her. For me it was almost like living it again. It sent goosebumps up my spine and down my arms, but my sister just sat through it like she wasn't even seeing it. When it was over, all she could say was, "Your hair looks nice."

I thought, *That's all? My hair looks nice? How cold?* But then later it occurred to me that she was completely cold hearted when it comes to me. I couldn't understand why she was so hateful to me, so jealous. It upset me so much that I couldn't even sleep with the help of my Ativan.

A few days later my youngest brother stopped by and asked, "What have you been up to lately?"

I told him all about the revival at Greensboro and then we watched the tape. I fast-forwarded to the part where I was called up. He said nothing, but when I looked over, I saw a tear running down his face. I asked, "You okay?"

He said, "That is so touching, and believing like me, and knowing God is real." He turned to me. "God will show you. Just be patient."

I said, "I have to be. I have no choice."

He wanted to go next time, but I didn't know when that would be.

I got a part time job at a local grocery store. Money was running out. In the meantime, every day, I would pray. "God, show me the way, and give me peace. Take all the pain away, in the name of Jesus." The job was only part time, but it would slow the drain on my bank account until I could find something better.

One day less than two weeks after I'd started, the manager comes out to me and tells me to leave. Even though I asked, he wouldn't tell me why, so I left. I was so upset and confused, and that was making my hyper spike really bad.

When I got home, I called my friend from the revival, but she couldn't talk then. She called back a few days later and I asked her, "Do you know anyone who knows anything about evil, or if someone has worked evil or had evil worked on them?"

I wasn't even sure she would understand the question, let alone if I'd asked it right, but she surprised me by saying, "Yes." She said she knew a man, and she would give him a call, and tell him my name and ask him to check me out.

I thought, *Okay. That was simple enough.*

She told me she would get back in touch real soon, after she heard back from him. She said he had a powerful gift as a healer, but she also told me that he stayed very busy helping folks all over the world. She knew him well.

This all sounded kind of out there, but I was desperate, so I would wait—again.

A couple weeks later she called me back and told me that her healer friend said someone has worked evil on me, and that he would be helping me.

I thought, *Okay, so what now?* I was spending longer and longer in the tub. I'd be in there all afternoon long, every day. I lived in that tub.

One night, right after I went to bed and wasn't asleep yet, I heard a big sound like a strong gush of wind in the bathroom. I went to investigate and there on the counter was a pile of black dirt. I had just been in here. I clean like a maniac every day. And here was a pile of dirt. I swept it off onto a tissue and flushed it down the toilet, and went back to bed.

The next morning, I got to thinking. *What had happened last night?* I had a strong feeling that it must have been this healer man checking on me, but I really didn't know.

I called up my friend and told her what happened. She told me it was the healer. She also told me to read Psalm 27 every day. So I did.

"The Lord is my light and my salvation; whom shall I fear? The Lord is the strength of my life; of whom shall I be afraid? **2** When the wicked, even mine enemies and my foes, came upon me to eat up my flesh, they stumbled and fell. **3** Though a host should encamp against me, my heart shall not fear: though war should rise against me, in this will I be confident. **4** One thing have I desired of the Lord, that will I seek after; that I may dwell in the house of the Lord all the days of my life, to behold the beauty of the Lord, and to enquire in his temple. **5** For in the time of trouble he shall hide me in his pavilion: in the secret of his tabernacle shall he hide me; he shall set me up upon a rock. **6** And now shall mine head be lifted up above mine enemies round about me: therefore, will I offer in his tabernacle sacrifices of joy; I will sing, yea, I will sing praises unto the Lord."

I also had a CD with the song, *Take it to the Lord.* I never had much of a voice to sing, but I played that CD and sang along, making a joyful noise, as the bible says. I really love that song.

I told my friend what I was doing, spending hours on end in the tub, reading from the bible, and singing along with my CD.

She told me to keep it up. She said the healer had told her that someone had worked some witchcraft on me. That it was tying me up.

I asked if it was on me or in me. I knew I had been through a lot, but was I strong enough and smart enough to listen and do what needed to be done? Would I know what to do and when to do it? I prayed hard that I was, in the name of Jesus.

Chapter 8

This went on for two months, from March until April of 2000.

One day my friend called with instructions from the healer. I was to cut a slice off a potato and place it on my back, and do that with a new slice three different nights in a row. I was to wear this slice of potato for the whole night while I slept. So I went to the store and bought three potatoes and some cloth tape.

On Friday night, I put the first slice on my back, right by where it always hurt, and went to bed. I figured it would be hard sleeping with this cold wet thing on my back, but I slept.

When I got up the next morning, I went to the bathroom and pulled up my nightwear. I pulled off the tape and then started to remove the potato. It felt hot and it stuck to my skin. Pealing it away hurt like peeling away a layer of skin. When I finally got the slice of potato around to where I could see it, there was a very clear image of a lizard there, stuck by its back in the potato. I had to stare at it for a while to believe what I was seeing. The edges of the potato were all really dark, like instead of potato skin, it was a rim of dark, clotted, nasty blood, not just dark and clotted, but really nasty and black too, and there was a lizard there, I swear there was a lizard in the potato. It was almost beyond anything I could bring myself to believe, but I was looking at it with my own two eyes.

The saying goes, 'seeing is believing', but there are times when it's hard to believe what the eyes are seeing. This was one of those times.

Suddenly, my left eye felt like it had something in it. I don't know how; I was just standing in my bathroom looking at this unbelievable thing that had come out of my back. I put the potato and its grisly image down on a napkin and tried to get the whatever out of my eye, but I couldn't get it. I called my sister and asked her if she would take me to the medical center to get my eye checked.

She didn't live very far away, but she went on about how she had to clean her house. I was scared and frantic; my eye was hurting so much and watering like I was bawling, but only the one eye. I begged her to take me to the doctor, I mean I had to *beg* her to alter her house cleaning schedule and come help me—she didn't want to come.

She finally agreed and arrived fifteen minutes later; I showed her the potato. She asked where it had come from so I told her all I had done. She just made a face and said, "Throw it away." as if it was the most horrid of things and it might be diseased.

But I said I wouldn't; I had two more nights to go. She didn't say anything else about it.

She didn't say anything on the drive to the doctor either. She took me to Dr. Jones's Medical Center in King, not my eye doctor at Prime Care on University Parkway. I'm not sure why, Prime Care was much closer. Maybe it was because it was a Saturday, and she figured they'd be closed.

When we arrived, she asked me if I wanted her to come in with her. She's my sister, why would she feel the need to ask such a thing? What else was she going to do, just sit in the car? I said, "Yes, please," and we went in.

I explained to the lady doctor that I thought something was in my eye. She looked, but didn't see anything, and since my eye was really red by now, she said I had pinkeye, so she wrote me a prescription for eye drops. I knew that wasn't it, but I got my prescription.

When we reached my place again, I asked my oh-so-very-silent sister to please get me a two-liter bottle of Pepsi before she went home because I couldn't drive. She didn't say anything, like she didn't even hear. She just left without any offer of further help, or comment of concern. Inside I put my eye drops in. My eye was watering so bad, I'm not sure the drops had a chance, but they didn't help.

That night I placed another potato on my back and went to bed. After feeling bad all day because of my eye, I fell asleep quickly and slept all night long. This sleeping all night long was new to me, but I didn't think of that yet.

The next morning, it was not as difficult to remove the potato slice from my back, and when I got it around to where I could see it, I could still see the lizard, but it was not as clear as the first one. I put it on a napkin beside the first one—one more night to go.

My eye was not feeling better—something was in there, and it hurt so bad I could not see out of that eye. Even pulling my eyelid down over my lower eyelid didn't help. Whatever it was, it was really stuck up in there. I didn't feel I could see well enough to drive so I stayed home from church and hoped the medicine would help.

Once again, I was real tired from the pain in my eye, so after putting the third slice of potato on my back, I went to bed at nine and fell asleep fast—exhausted.

The next morning, what I took from my back was just an old potato, but there was still the faintest pale image right there in the center; if I hadn't been looking for it, I might have missed it, then I thought to look at my back—there was a scar there. It looked like a surgical scar, only I'd never had any kind of surgery. This was the Lord's surgery. It was over. I was sure of it. For the first time in a very long time, I didn't feel hyper.

I called my eye doctor and made an appointment for that afternoon. It was just a little way, so, with a hand over my eye, I managed to drive myself there. I explained to the doctor how I thought something was in my eye. I also told him about going to the medical center and how they'd given me eye drops for pinkeye.

He looked into my eye with a light and pulled my eyelid out and looked close, then with a q-tip he tried to lift something out of my eye. It hurt so much, he had to put pain drops in and try again. When he was sure he got it all, I asked what it was.

"I have never seen anything like this in anyone's eye before," he said. He showed me. It was some black shiny jelled something about the size of a dime, and it was gooey with sticky slime. It almost made me gag just looking at it. He tossed the q-tip in the trash and put pain drops in my eye and covered it with a patch. He told me to keep the patch on for three days, and call him if my eye didn't get better.

Three days later, I took the patch off. My eye had drained a bunch of yellowish goo into the patch, but it felt good as new, well almost. It felt a little irritated so I just used over-the-counter drops for some relief. The only thing left is a brown discoloration on the outside of my eye, unnoticeable unless I point it out. I called my doctor and told him so; I wanted to thank him for getting that thing – whatever it was – out of my eye.

In 2009 I went to a new eye doctor and she took lots of pictures of my eye, then she gave me some medicine called generic tobramy cindexamethasone. After putting that in my eye, the next morning it felt like I had new eyes. They had been infected for years.

The month of March was I-can't-believe-it month for me. My hyper franticness was gone; the habit was still there, but the irresistible drive or push to just gogogo was no longer there. It was like learning how to breathe again; it was such a fresh feeling. I know it all happened. I have pictures to show, and I have a scar on my back from no man's surgery.

I called my friend from Walkertown and asked her what I was supposed to do with these potatoes and their poisonous lizard cargo. She told me she would call the healer and ask. Why she didn't let me call him, I don't know. Maybe he didn't want his number passed around to just anyone. Someone who could do what he'd done for me, I suppose he didn't have time for the millions of calls he would get if his number got around.

When she called back, she told me to take something silk, something I've worn, wrap the potatoes in it, and bury it all in the back yard.

I had a pretty black silk slip, my favorite, I hated to cut it up, but I did, and I tied those potatoes up in it. But now I needed to bury it only I didn't own a shovel. I called my sister. She asked me why I wanted a shovel, so I just told her I wanted to dig a hole; what else do you use a shovel for?

When I got over to her place, she asked me again, so I told her the whole thing. I got all riled up and went into all about this lizard being hurting in my back for twenty-one and a half years. She said nothing while I vented my feelings with, "Whoever did this, God will deal with them. It says in the bible, you can't do evil and get by with it." I told her, "I will find out who did this."

She just listened, saying nothing, looking into space like she didn't know what to say. I felt lost and confused. I needed someone to hear me out, to really listen to me, to believe me, even if just a little. And just in case you were wondering, she didn't offer to help her sister with the bad back dig this hole and rid herself of this curse. She couldn't be bothered.

I went back to my apartment and dug my hole. I was told to dig it deep enough so animals wouldn't find it and dig it up again.

Early the next morning, I took one last look at those potatoes. Yes, they were real. It had happened. Holding that silk package over my hole, I said a prayer. "I know you well, God, and you know me well too. I am a child of yours and you are the most loving God, and the only God I serve. You made me, and you saved me from the lizard taking my life. The doctor couldn't see it in his x-rays, but you saw it. I place this into your hands and I thank you now and I will thank you in the days to come, and I will serve you always, in Jesus' name. Amen." I put the package into the hole and covered it up good.

Now I needed to figure out how such a thing had gotten into my body. How did it all start? Who would do such a thing? But now I knew why I had been running like a machine on overdrive. I felt a lot better, but I wasn't great yet. The healing would take time, and there were so many things I simply had to relearn. I also wanted to see my doctor, just to talk, so I called and made an appointment.

I needed another job too, so I needed to get busy and get on with my life—I was so sick of this whole mess. I started searching the newspaper and saw a notice of a job fair to be held soon. On the morning I was going to go, I was eating bacon with my breakfast. I like crisp bacon, it wasn't hard, but suddenly the back of my front lower tooth just fell off. Now there was a hole there. I had always had good teeth, but now I had to go to the dentist. My appointment was for the following week.

The job fair didn't pan out so I signed up with a temporary service called Kelly Service and they called me up about a week later. I was to go for an interview with Xpedx Inc. owned by International Paper Company, as a switchboard operator. I was so excited; I dressed up very nice in my best professional outfit and went for my interview with this super nice manager. This was my first interview since being lizard-free and my hands weren't shaking. When the interview was over, he said he would get back with the service. A few days later, the service called—I got the job.

Being a switchboard operator, I had to be quick and learn who everyone was, and this was a big company so there were a lot of people to get to know. I had to think fast, but it didn't take me long to get the calls answered correctly and transferred to the proper person. It was a fast paced switchboard and there were other things to handle as well. There were also walk-ins from other companies looking to set up an appointment with someone to sell or buy; I had to be on the ball from eight in the morning until five in the evening. It felt so good to be back in the real world, helping myself and earning some good pay. My boss seemed to be very pleased with me. It didn't take him long to offer me the job full-time with better pay.

I finally got my bottom tooth built back up. It cost me $340, but by the grace of God, I managed to have the money to pay for it.

When I finally got in to talk to my doctor, I told him all I had been through and that the prophet had told me it had been going on for twenty-one and a half years, and it had been—I could see that now. All that chaos, all that hyper, for so long. Boy was he shocked. He immediately said, "Allison, let me pray with you." He took my hands and held them and said a very nice prayer thanking God for his help.

I then asked if I could show him my scar. He looked at it real close and said, "Allison, folks are so mean in this mixed-up world, but thank God and your healer for taking care of your back."

158

I told him I didn't feel the need to take the Ativan anymore at night. It was still hard to fall asleep, but not nearly as bad as it used to be. Then I told him about my new job and about sitting and not needing to move fast all the time. I also told him how my back was feeling stiff all the time now and how it felt weird and hollow in there, and I asked if he could send me over to the hospital sometime for an MRI or x-rays, it would have to be after my insurance kicked in, but he said he'd schedule them soon.

About a month later, I took my MRI report over to my doctor so he could explain it to me. He told me, the report said that I had five different areas in my lower back that were degenerated, and that it wasn't something that would get better. He said careful exercise and rest would ease the pain, and he recommended swimming as the perfect kind of exercise.

I wasn't so pleased with that news, but I continued to pray for God to show me who had worked this evil on me and why. I needed some answers to ease my mind. God had gotten me this far. He would show me the rest of the picture in His time.

Every day, after work, I watched the video of the revival and thought hard about what the prophet told me. This was a very strange time for me. It was like I was being reborn. I needed to find a path for my future and I wasn't used to such planning. All I'd done for so many years was scramble from job to job, from one place to live to another, barely taking the time to rest my head before bouncing on to the next thing. One thing I thought on was that I wanted to know more about God. I had always been a church-going person, but it occurred to me that of late it had only been one of those places where I'd land for a moment before taking off to the next. That wasn't what I consider going to church.

I stopped taking turns with my sister driving to her church out in Pfafftown and started attending a much bigger church much closer to home.

Going to church near home, while I really liked the place and the pastor, had its hazards. I started running into old friends and coworkers. You might think these meetings would be joyous, but in reality, it was rather hard. The questions were very nearly always the same. What have you been doing all these years? Are you married? Do you have any kids? All these questions remind me of all the years I had lost. Everyone I met these days, they were all married, had a kid or three, been divorced, had a life. I was starting over, and not from some failed marriage. I simply couldn't tell them where I'd been all these years, because I hadn't been anywhere and they wouldn't understand; they couldn't.

Meeting these people though reminded me of past friends, friends whose life I'd dropped out of, friends I really wanted to stay in touch with. There was my best friend from school. We had been so close back then. That kind of friendship was worth giving another chance. I found her number and gave her a call. It was so good to hear her voice and to do a little catching up; I wanted more. I decided to invite her to the beach for a long weekend on my dime.

She had a boyfriend, so after thinking about it for a little while, she offered that he could drive us there. It was a hot day in May and it was bike week. We had so much fun looking at all the bikers riding up and down the strip. I honestly can't remember having this much fun in a very long time. I remember laughing at times before, but that seemed like staged sound effects compared to this down-deep-in-the-heart laughing I was enjoying with my friend.

We found flea markets and looked at all the amazing things. We got some good sun and played in the salt water, which was good for my back.

I shared with her all that had happened with me, and showed her my scar. I told her all the dirty details as best as

I could put them into words. She was amazed and shocked, but she listened close, and when we got back home, I showed her the photographs I'd taken of the potatoes and their incredible images. I don't expect everyone to believe completely. I know how incredible this all sounds, but she listened, and she stayed. We continue to keep in touch. She's a grandmother now.

Following my doctor's orders, I spent a lot of time at the pool, and I usually wasn't the only person there. One day I noticed a good-looking man there. I noticed because he instantly looked away when I looked in his direction and I saw.

Eventually he got brave and we started talking. He told me he'd just gone through a bad marriage and didn't really trust women. I told him I'd been through enough wars just dealing with life, and yes, trust was a big deal with me too. I also kidded him about staring at me and then looking away when I looked. He just laughed it off. He was a nut sometimes, but I felt good about him.

Soon he took to leaving love notes on my door. He lived two buildings over and he had a boxer. I was scared of her at first, boxers are such powerful dogs, but when she got to know me, she wanted to stay in my apartment more than his.

We hung out a lot that summer by the pool; he loved to swim. He had a good-paying job, but as time went on we both were having a hard time paying the bills. We decided we'd get a two-bedroom apartment together and share the load.

Living with another person was hard for me. I'd struggled so hard to stand on my own two feet, it almost felt like I wasn't doing that anymore, even though the only thing we really shared was the utilities bills and the rent. He was a great roommate. He was neat and clean, and he helped out and was very thoughtful.

One day my youngest brother called and asked if I'd stop by after work; he hadn't seen me in a long time. When I got there, he took one look at me and said, "What have you done? You seem so different now."

I wasn't sure how to answer him. "You wouldn't believe me if I told you."

He wasn't going to take that for an answer, so I told him about the lizard, and I reminded him how the prophet had said evil had been worked on me twenty-one and a half years ago. I told him how all that time I had been so hyper and panicky and tired but couldn't sleep, and then I told him about how the healer had taken the lizard out of my back. I even showed him how my hands weren't shaking anymore. Then I showed him my scar.

He was understandably shocked; it is a horrible story, and I knew it sounded crazy, but he just looked at me and said, "You aren't so fast-moving anymore, and when you talk, it's much slower. I can talk to you now without you rushing off before I say two words."

I felt so bad when he told me that. I knew I was bad, rushing around all the time, but I just wasn't aware of what I might look like from the outside. "Tell me how I was back then."

He said, "Sister, you were hard to deal with. You were rude and thoughtless sometimes. I showed you two necklaces I'd bought for my wife and her mom, and you said something really hurtful."

I almost cried hearing that. "I'm so sorry. I honestly don't remember being so rude. Please forgive me." I went directly in and found his wife and I apologized to her face.

She said, "I know you have a good heart, and that you are a kind person, but you were very hard to deal with."

I told her, "That wasn't me, not the real me. The real Allison is here now."

My brother asked me if anyone else knew. I told them not to tell anyone. The kids were young and they wouldn't understand. The others knew I was acting all strange, but they didn't know why.

My brother asked if my sister knew. I couldn't keep anything from him. I told him, "Yes, she knows all about it." I told him about showing her the potatoes with the lizard.

He asked, "What did she say?"

I told him that she just said to throw it in the trash, and then I went on to tell him all the things I thought she should have done, knowing what she knew, that she never even offered to do. I told him all about the things she *did* do that I thought were so strange and out of place. As I think back on all that I'd said, it was still incomplete; I hadn't put it all together yet, but it was a start.

My brother was upset and even mad, but he went on to tell me the profound difference he saw in me. "Your eyes weren't shifting around all the time, and your skin doesn't look so sallow and gray."

I told him how dad always thought I was on some kind of drugs, and if I looked like that, I guess that was understandable now.

He said, "Dad didn't know what was going on with you and neither did we. At times we just dreaded seeing you, because you acted so crazy-hyper."

I told them I was in God's hands now and he would show me the way, and that one day, when I was ready, he would show me who had done this evil to me. I had no doubt, no doubt at all.

I went on to tell him all about my new job and my new boyfriend. I told him how good it felt to be busy, but not be so hyper, how I was getting so I could stand the interstate some, but that it would take some getting used to. I explained how tall buildings used to feel so huge and overpowering, but that now they were just big buildings, nothing more.

My brother was happy for me, but being my brother, he also told me not to jump the gun with the new guy. Give myself time to heal.

I heard him, but I didn't listen. I wanted to jump back into life with both feet and hit the ground running. I still had some things to learn, not to walk so fast, not to drive so slow, talk slower, look at the person I was talking to, listen to what they had to say—all of it, but I was more than ready to tackle all of that and more. I was ready to have a life.

166

Chapter 9

Eventually, my boyfriend and I moved across town to another two-bedroom apartment closer to where I work. It was in a much better area too, and had a nice pool and tennis courts, and plenty of space to take Chance, the boxer, for her walks. By now, I really loved that dog. I would take her for rides and walks, and sometimes the boyfriend got to come along.

Need I say, my sister didn't like him. They'd met once at church, and she was nice to him there, so he was all for going over to her house when she and her husband invited us. That was a mistake; I had never seen my sister act so badly. It seemed that all they could say was really bad jokes—hurtful things. Considering the mixed company, they weren't funny at all.

We put up with it as long as we could, but as soon as we could, we left. Almost the first thing my boyfriend said was, "Your sister acted so Ms. Holy Saint at church, but boy, was she different at home."

I told him all about the lizard in my back and how she'd known all my troubles, but would never talk to me about it.

He told me it sounded like she was jealous of me and didn't want me to be happy or have a life. He even told her so over the phone once. Boy, did she get mad.

A little while later, my sister said, "I had to keep my husband home, he was going to come over and shoot him."

Oh, that made me so mad. I said, "Why didn't you let him. He might have had his gun shoved where the sun doesn't shine."

My boyfriend didn't like me going over to see her, but, even though he was probably right about it all, she was still my sister, so I'd go anyway.

I guess he was trying to protect me, but I couldn't see it that way back then. Whenever I came back from her place, he'd give me living hell about it. He would call me lizard woman, trying his best to make me mad, saying my sister was behind it all, and I shouldn't be around her.

Sometimes I still get all in a hurry; it's like you're used to driving a hundred miles an hour for the longest time and suddenly you have to drive only about twenty-five miles an hour—it seems so slow, and you forget once in a while. Sometimes I wonder how my heart stood up to the demand.

One day when my boyfriend and I were shopping, I still had trouble remembering to slow down and be careful.

I stepped off the sidewalk to cross the street and forgot to look both ways. A huge city bus was coming up right in front of us. My boyfriend – thank God he was there – he grabbed my shirt and pulled me back out of the way. If he hadn't been there, I would have been killed. I had to go sit down for a while; I was so upset.

It was coming on winter, and pretty much all of a sudden, I couldn't walk very well. First the tops of my feet hurt so very badly I could scarcely stand. I'd walk all bent over sometimes, wondering when I would start feeling better. When the pain spread to the bottoms of my feet, and to my heels, I went to a foot doctor and he took some x-rays and told me I had heel spurs growing in my feet and that they needed to be cut out real soon. He gave me cortisone shots in both my heels, which hurt worse than the spurs, and then he gave me some special boots to wear that came all the way up to my knees. It was so hard getting them on and off with pants so I took to wearing dresses. Wearing boots during the winter wasn't so bad, but wearing dresses was the worst.

My boyfriend helped me with everything. He'd go warm up the car and carry things in and out for me. He'd go do all the shopping and help me walk up and down the

169

stairs. He was very good to me during those pain-filled days.

One Saturday, I decided I wanted to see what I could find at a health food store, so my boyfriend took me. He told me they wouldn't know what to do, but I wanted to see anyway.

There was a foreign-looking man there and I asked him if he knew any old remedies for heel spurs, and right off he said, "Yes. Go to the drug store and by some iodine and put it on your heels every night, then put on a pair of footsies and go to bed. Give it some time and they'll go away."

I did what the man said. It certainly couldn't hurt, and it just might help, and it was a lot less expensive than surgery. The way I saw it, it was worth a try.

My boyfriend fussed at me every night, saying I was using too much iodine, and that it was bad for me. It took about a month, but then I didn't need the boots anymore, and my heels no longer hurt. I went to the doctor and told him what I'd done; he just looked at me like I'd lost my mind.

I was always praying too, every day and every night. You can't tell me God doesn't heal. He does, all the time.

My sister and her boyfriend got married in 2002 and they built a pretty big house. That July they invited everyone over for a cookout on the 4th. My boyfriend didn't want me to go, but he also didn't want me to go alone so we went together.

It was a nightmare. What a wreck of an evening. Lots of my sister's new husband's family and friends were there. I didn't know anyone, and soon learned that I didn't like anyone there either, but we made the best of it.

When it was over, it seemed like my boyfriend and I simply couldn't say anything to each other unless it was something rude or crude or unkind. Later, I found out that lots of the people who were at that party got real sick; some even passed away not long after, but I wasn't thinking of that—I should have paid attention though. Seems like every time I should have paid attention, I didn't.

In 2003 my boyfriend and I decided things would be easier if we bought our own home, so in July we moved in, but life with my boyfriend only got worse, though we weathered it as best we could. His mother never liked me. She preferred his ex-wife and always treated me as the intruder.

For the 4th of July of 2004, my sister and her husband had a cookout, but by then things were so bad between my boyfriend and I that though we went, we didn't stay together much longer after. In fact, my life fell all to pieces shortly after that party. Chance, the boxer, died, my boyfriend and I broke up and he moved out to become a truck driver, leaving me with the house, and my job ended when they automated the switchboard. They'd downsized a lot that year so there was just no place for me—all before the end of the month.

Back to the unemployment line for me.

Shortly after my boyfriend moved out, my sister and her husband came over. She looked around with her imperious air and said, "Sell the place."

I thought, *Why would I?* But still it was a really big load to try to carry on my own, what with me no longer working.

About my boyfriend, my sister tried to comfort me by saying, "I told you he wasn't any good."

Well, no. She never said those words. All she ever did was make it completely clear that she didn't like him. Her husband told me much the same thing one day at church, but there's no way he could form any kind of opinion about the guy, he'd only seen him those few times we went to their place, and they never even talked much then. You really don't learn anything about anyone if all you do is insult them. Yeah, lots of comfort for my broken heart coming from that direction.

So here I am, no job and no boyfriend, and he even took the riding lawnmower back to Sears, so I was stuck with a $905 house payment while trying to sell the place and I had to keep it looking nice. That meant hours of mowing the yard with an old push mower that wouldn't start most of the time. Mowing the yard consumed my Saturdays. I did eventually find a used riding mower I could afford; that helped a lot, cutting my Saturday in the yard in half.

To pay the house payment, I found another full time job in January of 2005, and I found a part time job in March, which made my weekdays too long to even count as days. I'd get up so I could be at work at eight in the morning and then not get home until half past ten at night to fall in bed, my day gone. Good thing the bank was looking hard for a buyer, because I couldn't keep this up for long.

My old boyfriend called once, saying how sorry he was and that I was so much better to him than his ex-wife or anyone had ever been. He told me he loved me and wanted us to get back together, but I had no trust for him now. I did accept his apology and wished him the best in life.

One day at work, it felt like the bottom of my mouth was suddenly full of gravel. It didn't hurt so much, but it was making the underside of my tongue raw, so I went to look, and I couldn't believe what I was seeing. It looked like bones were growing out of my jaw, under my tongue. This was scary; I'd never seen or heard of such a thing, so I showed my boss, and he said to call my dentist. They could take me in right away, so he let me off to go see him.

My dentist sent me over to an oral surgeon to get it taken care of as soon as possible. The appointment was for a week later, and my youngest brother, his wife, and my middle brother all went with me to the appointment. They were upset and concerned for me. I did show my sister, but she couldn't look at it. She wasn't there for my appointment.

The doctor told me that it would be surgery and that I would be put to sleep for the work, so I would need someone to drive me home after. Well, I had three drivers, so I guess my sister thought I didn't need another one.

I was so scared; I prayed to God, asking for his protection, wondering how this could have happened to me.

All I could think of was that this must be more of the lizard coming out of me. He was in my back to control everything I did, in my eye to control what I saw, in my heels to control my path, and now in my mouth, maybe to control what I said. Was there going to be more? I prayed to God that he would find all of it. I would take whatever it was as long as he got it all out of me.

When the doctor was done, he told me he had to cut the bone to get them all out, but he got all of them. He also told me that they were pearl white, and that he'd never seen anything like it before. I didn't tell him all the rest I'd been through. He probably wouldn't believe me.

Work went back to normal, but as the year got colder, I got stiffer. By October I couldn't straighten my leg or put my right foot on the ground. My doctor said it was arthritis, and that no surgery would be necessary, but I would need physical therapy.

Physical therapy ended up being too painful too, so the doctor gave me some medicine for inflammation, but that didn't help either. The pain was so severe all in my hip and down my leg that it got to the point where I couldn't get around at all. I'd sit, and then I couldn't stand up after. I would get stuck trying to walk. It takes two legs to walk, and if one just won't go forward, then there's no walking.

My doctor told me I would be like this for the rest of my life—that there just wasn't anything to be done, but he referred me to another doctor for a hip injection. I had to look that up in the dictionary, and *oh* it sounded horrible, but this pain was horrible too, so maybe it would make things more tolerable.

I got my first hip injection in February of 2006, and the doctor told me to rest for that day. I went back to work the next day, but then I was back to using a cane and being stuck, and the doctor told me I wasn't supposed to be getting another injection for six weeks. I ended up getting a hip replacement in April.

God took care of me though. The doctor told me I would end up using two units of blood. I told the doctor that morning that I had brought the angels and the Lord with me, and the Lord was a great physician, and he would be working through his hands.

When I woke up after the surgery, my sister-in-law said the surgeon didn't use anyone's blood but mine. What a miracle! I just started thanking the Lord and praying in Jesus' name.

After I got home, I took things easy, but I could move again. My sister came and stayed with me for two days, much to my surprise. That was the second time she did something like that in all the years we'd been together. She said once, "You, Allison, have been through so much. I couldn't have gone through all you have."

As close as we have always been, she *should* know. I thought, *You just don't care to know.* I said, "God will show me who did all this evil on me, and as soon as I figure it all out, I'm going to write a book."

My sister just scoffed. "Okay, you write your book."

I spent twelve weeks at home, and after my sister spent her two nights here, I was all alone. She'd come by on Saturdays to put TV dinners in my freezer, but she never offered to see if I needed or wanted to go anywhere, not even to church. She only lived two and a half miles away, but she couldn't be bothered with the extra fifteen minutes of her time to check in on me.

By the time my convalescence was up, I could mow my yard again. My hip still feels stiff when it rains, but I suppose everyone has to be able to predict the weather somehow at some point in their life. I go to the YMCA and walk in the water for a while, or take a hot shower. I have come a very long way, by the grace of God.

Day after day, I wondered who could have done this to me. I had seen the evidence, but I could not fathom such an enemy. Who had I made so angry that they would want to curse me? I just couldn't understand why. I had to think back, back before all the fog and confusion, and try to piece things together like a puzzle. It was so hard.

I asked the healer if he knew, but he refused to give me a straight answer; it wasn't his place to direct my anger. It was God's will that I wait a little longer, to think a little harder on all these things.

Sometimes I would mention to my sister, "Whoever did this to me will pay. I will find out someday."

She never answered. Her face would just go blank, as if she was saying, "So," but wasn't saying it out loud.

Sometimes I would get so angry thinking back on all the things I had been denied. I used to go out nights. I should have found a good husband and raised a family by now. It was a good thing I didn't have a baby; who knows what that lizard would have done to such an innocent bit of life? Just trying could have killed me and the baby. That's what they wanted, whoever started this; they wanted me dead, but why? That was the big puzzle. People hurt people out of hate, or just malicious evil, and I couldn't think of anyone who fit that description. I couldn't think of anyone who hated me so much that they would want to torture me for half my life, or even wish me dead.

Back at work, I was no longer a parking enforcement officer; I was now working in a parking deck collecting money from people who wanted to park their cars in the city parking deck. That was fine with me. I gave up my part time job over at the Forsyth Medical Center; it was just too much for me. I was still healing in my hip, and mentally trying to keep things together and figure things out.

I had always been a happy child, but now it was very hard for me to find something to be happy about, and I just didn't want to spend time with others either.

My middle brother would come stay with me sometimes. He had his own problems, but I didn't mind the company. He was a loving and kind man. He was divorced, and like our dad, he didn't have a lot to say.

I told him about the lizard and everything I'd learned since, and prayed for.

He said, "Keep praying. God will give you the answers you are looking for in time." The worst thing he said about the whole thing was, "Whoever did this will pay, and spit on them."

I thought, *I wouldn't spit on them if they were on fire.*

In April of 2007, I got a promotion to a new department that had opened up recently, but I never got the feeling of fitting in much; it was like I was being left behind, or maybe I was willing myself to be left out. I really couldn't say. One very good thing that happened to me was a lady over in Rural Hall gave me a beagle/lab pup, and he was such a happy companion. All that happy just had to rub off. I named him Roscoe Walls. He was very smart and easy to house-train, and he was my best friend instantly. He had a gentle energy that got me out there. He'd get me out walking, and be so happy to see people, and I needed that, all of it.

I'd take him to work with me. We'd stop by McDonald's for breakfast, and then to work. I made him a nice bed in the car, and then go check on him during breaks. My hours were from six in the morning until two in the afternoon, so we weren't there all day long.

One day my boss called me up. "Allison, do you have your dog in the building with you?"

I said, "I don't have a dog here. He's my little human with a fur coat."

I heard a big burst of laughter on the other end of the phone. "Oh, just wanted to make sure you didn't bring your dog."

"Oh no," I said. I was laughing now too. "No way. I wouldn't do that."

By December, I just couldn't take the job any more. My back and hip bothered me something terrible. Thirty years I'd been working and not much to show for it, just getting by.

Chapter 10

One day in 2009, my sister called, wanting to go shopping at her favorite lady's store. I picked her up on Saturday afternoon, and who do you think we ran into at the store? Fat Boy's mom. I hadn't seen her since I worked with her at the Old Town Towel Shop, which seemed like ages ago now. I liked her; I wish she hadn't been Fat Boy's mom, but you can't have everything. We chatted along, catching up, and it came out that Fat Boy had been real sick for some years now and that his back was deteriorating and the doctor didn't know why.

Let me tell you, a light bulb went off in my mind. I didn't say anything to her; I just expressed sympathies for him that I didn't feel and felt really sorry for her.

When we got back in the car, I said, "I know now who did the evil on me. Would you like a lizard crawling all over you? I can't prove it, but time will tell."

Of course my sister's reply was, "Do you need to talk about this *again*?"

I couldn't believe my ears. This made me mad. Her friend had put me through hell, and she didn't want to talk about it. Worst of all, there was no surprise. *No surprise!*

She knew all along. *Now* I understood. *Now* I had the whole puzzle, *and* I bet she never said a thing to her husband about the lizard and everything. If she did, he might have put all the clues together too, and she couldn't have that.

I am so thankful to God for showing me the truth, all of it.

One Sunday in October of 2010, while we were at church, my cousin, who was a paramedic for the Old Richmond Fire Department, got a call and had to go. It seems something was done there or said there, and it got out that he was related to my sister, so he told her what had happened. He told her that Fat Boy had died of a bad heart attack and was dead before he hit the floor.

My sister called me the next morning and told me that she and her husband had gone over there to check up on Fat Boy's mom and see how she was holding up. Yes, Fat Boy had still been living with his mother all these years. She told me what had happened. That he had only just been home from the hospital for a few days, and that they'd used fourteen pints of blood for his surgery, but it didn't do him any good. The EMTs had said he'd died of a heart attack real sudden like.

I told her that I simply couldn't find it in my heart to feel sorry for him. I was sorry for all he had put his mom through, but that was as far as I was willing to go. My sister seemed so surprised, but I told her in plain words. "He was the one who put that curse on me, and when I didn't die, he talked you into abandoning me, so he could work his evil on me day after day. You never wanted to hear me talk about it because you already knew all about it. He is very evil, and if there is a hell – and I do believe there is – he is there for what he did to me for twenty-one and a half years. I simply can't believe you didn't know he was so evil, all the time you spent around him. If I hadn't prayed to the Lord, and if he hadn't led me to the people I needed to help me, I would have died, and no one would have known why. You of all people should know that when a curse is properly broken and put away, it goes back on the person who set the curse in the first place. Well, you have seen the proof of that. Fat Boy started to get sick ten years ago, right after I got that lizard out of my back. You saw it. You told me to just throw it away, but I didn't. Fat Boy was a dirty evil person and he is getting his just rewards now. And you will answer before God too, if you had anything at all to do with it."

My life goes on. Justice has and will be done, in His time, not mine. Now I must wrestle with myself, and my anger every day. Following the Lord's path is not always easy, but I shall prevail.

According to the King James Bible, "In remunerative justice he distributes rewards (James 1:12; 2 Tim. 4:8); in vindictive or punitive justice he inflicts punishment on account of transgression (2 Thess. 1:6)."

James 1:12 "Blessed is the man that endureth temptation: for when he is tried, he shall receive the crown of life, which the Lord hath promised to them that love him."

2 timothy 4:8 "Henceforth there is laid up for me a crown of righteousness, which the Lord, the righteous judge, shall give me at that day: and not to me only, but unto all them also that love his appearing."

2 Thessalonians 1:6 "Seeing it is a righteous thing with God to recompense tribulation to them that trouble you."

185

Allison Walls is a very real person and the practice of Voodoo is also very real. Allison is only one victim of such practices.

There is no real proof, nothing that will ever hold up in a court of law, but all the events recorded in this book happened, and the conjecture reached at the end is Allison's alone.

Kim,
Merry Christmas
Happy New Year!
Love,
Allison D. Walls